Scott Foresman - Addison Wesley

Alternative Lessons
Reteaching Workbook

Grade 6

Scott Foresman - Addison Wesley

Editorial Offices: Glenview, Illinois • New York, New York
Sales Offices: Reading, Massachusetts • Duluth, Georgia • Glenview, Illinois
Carrollton, Texas • Menlo Park, California

http://www.sf.aw.com

Overview

Alternative Lessons (Reteaching Workbook) provide additional teaching options for teachers to use with students who have not yet mastered key skills and concepts covered in the student text. These also can serve as worksheets for students who have missed class when the original lesson was presented. Substitute teachers may also use these as independent lessons whenever necessary.

An Alternative Lesson is provided for each regular lesson in the student text. Each lesson is broken into sections labeled *Example* and *Try It.*

Example consists of worked-out examples of important concepts that mirror those taught in the student text. In addition, key definitions necessary for students' understanding are included whenever applicable. Reading is kept to a minimum to help students follow the steps used in finding the answers.

Try It often uses guided practice for the first exercise to enhance the students' understanding of the different steps that are involved in finding the answer to the exercise. This is followed by similar exercises that give students an opportunity to apply what they have learned.

ISBN 0–201–46082-3

Copyright © Addison Wesley Longman, Inc.

Printed in the United States of America

3 4 5 6 7 8 9 10 – V004 – 10 09 08 07 06 05

Contents

Chapter 10: Ratio, Proportion, and Percent

Chapter 11: Solids and Measurement

Chapter 12: Probability

Reading Graphs

A **pictograph** uses symbols to represent data. A **bar graph** uses vertical or horizontal bars to display numerical information. The two graphs below show the same data.

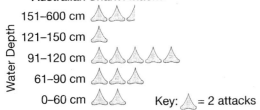

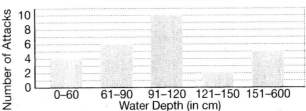

━━ Example 1 ━━

Use the pictograph to decide how many shark attacks occur at a water depth of 61–90 cm.

Step 1: Count the number of symbols beside the bar marked 61–90 cm. There are 3 symbols.

Step 2: Multiply the number of symbols and the number each symbol represents. The key shows that each symbol equals 2 shark attacks, so find $3 \times 2 = 6$.

Six shark attacks occur at a water depth of 61–90 cm.

━━ Example 2 ━━

Use the bar graph to decide how many shark attacks occur at a water depth of 61–90 cm.

Step 1: Find the bar labeled 61–90 cm on the horizontal scale showing water depths.

Step 2: Find the number on the vertical scale that matches the top of the bar: 6.

Six shark attacks occur at a water depth of 91–120 cm.

Try It Use the pictograph to answer each question. Then use the bar graph to verify each answer.

a. How many shark attacks occur at a water depth of 0–60 cm? _____

b. How many shark attacks occur at a water depth of 151–600 cm? _____

c. At what water depth did the least number of attacks occur? _____

d. How many more attacks occur at a depth of

   61–90 cm than occur at a depth of 0–60 cm? _____

e. Which graph did you find easier to use? Why?

Name _____

Misleading Graphs

There are many ways to make a graph that can mislead a careless reader. One way is to start labeling the graph at a number other than zero without indicating that some numbers have been skipped. A graph can mislead by lengthening or shortening the space between data values in order to give a certain impression.

▬ Example ▬

Does *Sports Action* cost 4 times as much as *In Fashion?* Explain.

The bar showing the cost of *Sports Action* is about 4 times the length of the bar showing the cost of *In Fashion.* Look carefully at the scale along the left axis of the graph. Notice that the scale starts at $50 so the first $50 of each magazine subscription has been skipped. The graph is misleading.

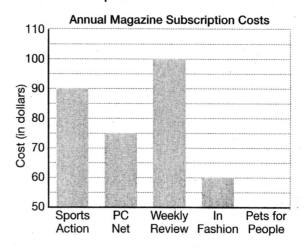

The *Sports Action* subscription is $90 per year. *In Fashion* costs $60 per year. Since 90 is not 4 times as much as 60, *Sports Action* does not cost 4 times as much as *In Fashion.*

Try It

a. *Weekly Review* looks like it costs 5 times as much as *In Fashion.*

What is the yearly cost for *Weekly Review*? _____ For *In Fashion*? _____

Does *Weekly Review* cost 5 times as much as *In Fashion*? Explain.

_____

b. *Weekly Review* looks like it costs _____ times as much as *PC Net.*

What is the yearly cost for *Weekly Review*? _____ For *PC Net*? _____

Is this a true or false impression? _____

c. Add a bar to the graph to show that a new magazine, *Pets for People,* costs $80 for a year's subscription.

d. *Pets for People* looks like it costs _____ times as much as *In Fashion.*

Is this a true or false impression? _____

e. What can you do to the graph so that it is not misleading?

_____

Scatterplots and Trends

A **scatterplot** shows paired data. Each point on a scatterplot represents *two* data values. Sometimes the points in a scatterplot suggest a relationship between two sets of data that shows a pattern. This relationship is called a **trend.**

 Example

How long does it take Product *A* to cook in the microwave? How long does it take to cook in the oven?

Step 1: Find *A*. Go right to 3 minutes. This is the point on the horizontal axis that is below Point *A*.

Step 2: Find *A*. Go up to 25 minutes. This is the point on the vertical axis that is to the left of Point *A*.

Product *A* cooks for 3 minutes in the microwave and 25 minutes in the oven.

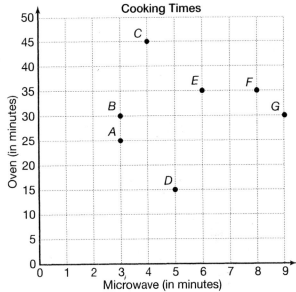

Try It

Using the scatterplot, find the following information.

a. The time it takes Product *B* to cook in a microwave _____

b. The time it takes Product *B* to cook in an oven _____

c. The product that cooks for 15 minutes in the oven _____

d. The time it takes Product *C* to cook in a microwave _____

e. The time it takes Product *E* to cook in an oven _____

f. The product that cooks for 45 minutes in the oven _____

g. How much longer it takes Product *G*

than Product *D* to cook in an oven _____

h. A product takes 40 minutes to cook in an oven. Do you think it would take more or less time to cook in the microwave? Explain.

_____

_____

Tallies, Frequency Charts, and Line Plots

Tallies are marks that help to organize a large set of data. Each tally mark indicates one time that the value appeared in the data.

A **frequency chart** can help you list the data quickly. Each value that appeared in the data is followed by the number of times it appeared.

▬ Example ▬

Use the data to make a frequency chart.
How many words have 4 letters?

> Number of Letters in Each Word in a Given Paragraph
> 8, 3, 4, 2, 3, 2, 3, 5, 4, 1, 9, 5, 3, 1, 4, 4

Step 1: List the number of letters in order from 1 to 9.

Step 2: Record a tally mark for each item. Place a tally mark next to 8. Do this for each of the data.

Step 3: Count the tally marks to find the frequency of each item. There are two tallies next to 1, so the frequency is 2. Do this for every item.

Since there are 4 tallies for words with 4 letters, there are 4 words that contained 4 letters.

Number of Words

Number of letters	Tally marks	Frequency
1	||	2
2	||	2
3	||||	4
4	||||	4
5	||	2
6		0
7		0
8	|	1
9	|	1

Try It Use the data to make a frequency chart. How many sentences in the short story have 13 words?

> Number of Words in 12 Sentences
> 12, 11, 10, 13, 8, 13, 10, 9, 7, 8, 7, 10

Number of Sentences

Number of words	Tally marks	Frequency

a. Record a tally mark for the number of words in each sentence.

b. Total the tallies and write the frequency for each sentence length.

c. How many sentences have 13 words? _____

Scales and Bar Graphs

A bar graph is a way to visually display and compare numerical data. The **scale** of a bar graph is the "ruler" that measures the heights of the bars. The **intervals** are the equal divisions marked on the scale to make it easier to read. The lines on which a bar graph is built are the **horizontal axis** and the **vertical axis**. The **range** of a data set refers to the difference between the highest value and the lowest value.

▬ Example ▬▬▬▬▬

Sam followed these steps to make a bar graph using the data on mountain heights.

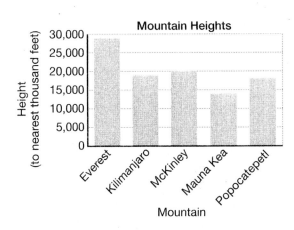

Step 1: He used a scale from 0 to 30,000 since the highest mountain was 29,000 feet. The range of data is 15,000. He used intervals of 5,000 because 30,000 is divisible by 5,000.

Step 2: He drew bars to represent the data and labeled the bars.

Step 3: He wrote a title for the graph.

Try It Use the data to complete the bar graph.

Ocean Depths (to nearest thousand meters)

Ocean	Depth (m)
Arctic	6,000
Indian	7,000
Atlantic	9,000
Pacific	11,000

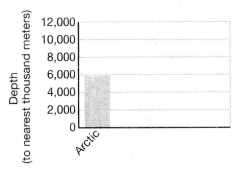

a. What is the range of the data? _____

b. What interval was used on the vertical scales? _____

c. Would it be reasonable to use an interval of 20,000? Explain.

_____

_____

d. Draw bars that represent the depths of the Indian, Pacific, and Atlantic oceans.

e. Label and shade the bars. Give the graph a title.

f. Write a problem that can be solved using the data in the graph.

_____

_____

Stem-and-Leaf Diagrams

A **stem-and-leaf diagram** is a graph that shows the shape of the data according to the data place values. The **"leaf"** of a number is usually the right-hand digit. The leaf is one digit. The **"stem"** is the portion of the number to the left of the leaf. The stem can be one or more digits.

▬ Example ▬

Make a stem-and-leaf diagram using the data showing minutes spent eating lunch.

Minutes Spent Eating Lunch
46, 35, 12, 37, 28, 10, 22, 54, 19, 13, 46, 51

Step 1: Decide what the stem of the diagram will represent. Since these data are two-digit numbers, the stem will be the tens digits and the leaves will be the ones digits.

Step 2: Write the tens digits in order in the left-hand column of the diagram. Then write each leaf at the right of its stem as they occur in the problem.

Step 3: Complete the second stem-and-leaf diagram, with the leaves in order from least to greatest.

Step 2

Stem	Leaf
1	2 0 9 3
2	8 2
3	5 7
4	6 6
5	4 1

Step 3

Stem	Leaf
1	0 2 3 9
2	2 8
3	5 7
4	6 6
5	1 4

Try It

a. Make a stem-and-leaf diagram of the data showing the monthly attendance at the teen club.

Attendance at Teen Club
489, 527, 479, 519, 514, 480, 493, 523, 508, 504

Step 2

Stem	Leaf

Step 3

Stem	Leaf

1. Write the stems in the left column. Since all of the data are in the 47s, 48s, 49s, 50s, 51s, and 52s, you need six stems.

2. For each number, write the last digit (the leaf) in the right column on the same line as the matching stem.

b. Make a stem-and-leaf diagram to show the data in this chart. Remember to put the leaves in order.

Sit-ups in One Minute
35, 28, 52, 58, 12, 29, 41, 37, 19, 23, 26, 45

Step 2

Stem	Leaf

Step 3

Stem	Leaf

Median and Mode

The **median** of a data set is the middle number when the data are listed from lowest to highest. If a set has two middle numbers, the median is the value halfway between the two middle numbers.

The **mode** of a data set is the item that occurs most often. If all items occur once, there is no mode. If several items occur "most often," each is a mode.

▬ Example ▬

Find the median age and the mode age of these children.

Child	Age	Child	Age
Kevin	2 years	Roberto	2 years
Jamal	3 years	Lauren	4 years
Andrea	$3\frac{1}{2}$ years	Althea	$1\frac{1}{2}$ years
Mariko	2 years	Jerry	3 years

Arrange the ages from lowest to highest.
The median age is $2\frac{1}{2}$ years because
it is halfway between 2 and 3.
The mode age is 2 years because
it is the number that occurs most frequently.

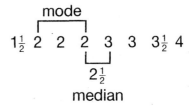

Try It   Find the median number of baseball cards and the mode number of baseball cards for the six members of the Baseball Fan Club.

Number of cards: 20, 53, 39, 41, 34, 41

a. Arrange the numbers in order from least to greatest. _____

b. What is the median number of cards? _____

c. What is the mode number of cards? _____

Find the median and mode for each set of data.

d. Age of Taxi Drivers: 23, 23, 78, 54, 56, 34, 78, 52, 34, 67

_____

e. Cost of Stereos: $384, $190, $827, $641, $384, $530, $773, $827, $299

_____

The Meaning of Mean

The **mean** of a data set is the sum of the items in the set divided by the number of items. The mean can also be called the *average.* To find the mean, add all the data values and divide by the number of values.

━━ Example ━━

The weekly allowances for a group of children are: $5.00, $4.00, $3.50, $6.00, $5.00, $2.50, $2.00, $7.00, $6.50, $4.50, $3.50, $5.50. What is the mean allowance? Round your answer to the nearest cent.

Step 1: Add all of the amounts.
The total is $55.00.

Step 2: There are 12 items.
Divide the total dollar amount by this number.
$55.00 ÷ 12 = $4.5833...

The mean allowance is $4.58 when rounded to the nearest cent.

Try It Find the mean price of these six boxes of crackers:
$3.25, $2.75, $2.00, $3.25, $2.50, $2.75.

a. Add all of the prices together. What is the sum? _____

b. How many boxes of crackers are there all together? _____

c. Divide the sum of the prices by the number of boxes of crackers.

Show your number sentence. _____ ÷ _____ = _____

d. Write the mean price. _____

Find the mean weight of these cats: Frisky, 6 lb; Mittens, 8 lb; Tiger, 12 lb; Baby Kitty, 7 lb; Patches, 10 lb; Kissy, 9 lb; Tripod, 14 lb; Angel, 9 lb. Round your answer to the nearest whole number.

e. Step 1: _____

f. Step 2: _____

g. Mean weight: _____

Find the mean of each set of data.

h. Length of these six pencils:
12 cm, 15 cm, 16 cm, 10 cm, 11 cm, 14 cm _____

i. Score of these eight tests:
78, 69, 82, 75, 90, 88, 72, 86 _____

The Effects of Outliers

An **outlier** is a number in a data set that is very different from the rest of the data. Outliers can have a big effect on the mean.

▬ Example ▬▬▬▬

Find the mean, median, and mode with and without the outlier for this set of data about the number of days 6 people exercised in one month: 4, 23, 21, 22, 21, 23.

Identify the outlier. Since most of data is in the low twenties, the outlier of the data set is 4.

Find the mean of the data set.
The mean is 19.

Think: $4 + 23 + 21 + 22 + 21 + 23 = 114$
$114 \div 6 = 19$

Without the outlier, 4, the mean of the data set is 22.

Think: $23 + 21 + 22 + 21 + 23 = 110$
$110 \div 5 = 22$

Find the median of the data set.
The median is 21.5.

Think: 4, 21, 21, 22, 23, 23
↓
21.5

Without the outlier, 4, the median of the data is 22.

Think: 21, 21, 22, 23, 23

Find the mode of the data set.
The modes are 21 and 23.

Think: 4, 21, 21, 22, 23, 23

Without the outlier, 4, the modes of the data remain the same, 21 and 23.

Think: 21, 21, 22, 23, 23

Try It Find the mean, median, and mode, with and without outliers for this set of data: 450, 420, 435, 450, 5500, 440, 425, 460.

a. Identify the outlier. _____

b. Organize your results in the table.

Miles Traveled Last Week		
	With Outlier	Without Outlier
Mean		
Median		
Mode		

Reading and Writing Large Numbers

Every digit of a number has a **place value.** The place value tells you
how much that digit represents.

━━ Example 1 ━━

Write 72,152,295 in word form.

Think:

	Place Value													
Trillions			Billions			Millions			Thousands			Ones		
H	T	O	H	T	O	H	T	O	H	T	O	H	T	O
							7	2	1	5	2	2	9	5

Write: seventy-two million, one hundred fifty-two thousand, two hundred ninety-five

So, 72,152,295 can be written as seventy-two million, one hundred
fifty-two thousand, two hundred ninety-five.

Try It Write in word form.

a. 8,039,183,702

_____

_____

b. 754,031,590,344,601

_____

_____

━━ Example 2 ━━

Write two hundred six billion, twelve thousand, fifty-six in standard form.

Think:

	Place Value													
Trillions			Billions			Millions			Thousands			Ones		
H	T	O	H	T	O	H	T	O	H	T	O	H	T	O
			2	0	6	0	0	0	0	1	2	0	5	6

Write: 206,000,012,056

So, two hundred six billion, twelve thousand, fifty-six can be written as 206,000,012,056.

Try It Write in standard form.

c. thirty-seven billion, six hundred
four million, one hundred fifteen _____

d. four hundred trillion, nine hundred fifty-six
billion, forty-four million, six hundred thousand. _____

e. two hundred million, five thousand, four _____

Rounding Large Numbers

Rounding is one way to find a number that's more convenient.
Rounding will give you the closest convenient number according to a
given place value.

▬ Example ▬▬▬

Round 82,439 to the nearest hundred.   8 2 4̲ 3 9

There are four steps involved in the rounding process:

Step 1: Find the place value.   The place value is "hundreds."

Step 2: Look at the digit to the right   The digit is 3.

Step 3: If this digit is 5 or greater, add one to
        the place-value digit. If it's less than
        5, leave the place-value digit alone.   3 is less than 5, so it will not change.

Step 4: Change the digits to the right to zeros. The rounded number is 82,400.

82,439 rounds to 82,400 when rounding to the nearest hundred.

Try It Round 132,874,015 to the nearest hundred-thousands.

a. The hundred-thousands digit is _____.

b. The digit to the right of the hundred-thousands is _____.

c. Is that digit 5 or greater? _____

d. Write the rounded number. Remember to change
     digits to the right of hundred-thousands to zeros. _____

Round each number to the given place.

e. 941 to the tens place _____

f. 103,555 to the thousands place _____

g. 1,806,090 to the ten-thousands place _____

h. 967,063,402 to the hundred-thousands place _____

i. 460,027,971 to the millions place _____

j. 457,032,333 to the ten-millions place _____

k. 384,203,670,159 to the ten-billions place _____

Comparing and Ordering Numbers

To compare two numbers with the same number of digits, start at the left and find the first place-value position that has different digits. The number with the larger digit is the larger number. The symbols > and < are used to compare numbers.

The symbol > means "is greater than."
The symbol < means "is less than."

▬ Example ▬

Compare 87,812 and 87,349.

The numbers have the same number of digits.
Start with the digit at the left.

Step 1:　 8̄ 7 8 1 2　　Compare the ten-thousands digits. They are equal.
　　　　　 8̄ 7 3 4 9　　Move to the right.

Step 2:　 8 7̄ 8 1 2　　Compare the thousands digits. They are equal.
　　　　　 8 7̄ 3 4 9　　Move to the right.

Step 3:　 8 7 8̄ 1 2　　Compare the hundreds digits. 8 is greater than 3.
　　　　　 8 7 3̄ 4 9

87,812 is greater than 87,349.
This can also be written as 87,812 > 87,349.

Try It　Compare 21,009 and 21,090.

a. Compare the digits, starting at the left.
In which place-value positions are the digits the same?

_____

b. For the first two digits that are not
the same, which number is larger? _____

c. Which is greater: 21,009 or 21,090? _____

d. Compare 6802 and 6820. Which is greater? _____

Compare the numbers, using > or <.

e. 45 _____ 54

f. 932 _____ 923

g. 5676 _____ 5675

h. 6321 _____ 6279

i. 11,122 _____ 11,211

j. 86,321 _____ 86,279

k. 120,932 _____ 102,923

l. 707,213 _____ 778,689

Exponents

When you multiply numbers, each number is a **factor** of the result. Repeated multiplication can be represented by using exponential notation. The **base** is the number to be multiplied. The **exponent** is the number that tells you how many times the base is used as a factor.

5 is the exponent.

$3 \times 3 \times 3 \times 3 \times 3 = 3^5$

5 factors   3 is the base.

━━ Example 1 ━━

Write $4 \times 4 \times 4$ using exponents.

The number to be multiplied is 4, so 4 will be the base.
The base is used as a factor 3 times, so 3 will be the exponent.

$4 \times 4 \times 4 = 4^3$

Try It Write $7 \times 7 \times 7 \times 7 \times 7 \times 7$ using exponents.

a. What is the base? _____   **b.** What is the exponent? _____

c. Write $7 \times 7 \times 7 \times 7 \times 7 \times 7$ using exponents. _____

Write using exponents.

d. $25 \times 25 \times 25$ _____   **e.** $6 \times 6 \times 6 \times 6 \times 6 \times 6 \times 6$ _____

f. $10 \times 10 \times 10 \times 10$ _____   **g.** $9 \times 9 \times 9 \times 9 \times 9 \times 9$ _____

━━ Example 2 ━━

Write 3^4 in expanded and standard forms.

The base is 3: It is the number being multiplied.
The exponent is 4: It is the number of times the base is multiplied.

In expanded form, $3^4 = 3 \times 3 \times 3 \times 3$.
In standard form, $3^4 = 81$.

Try It Write in expanded and standard forms.

	Expanded	Standard
h. 5^3	_____	_____
i. 4^4	_____	_____
j. 2^5	_____	_____

Mental Math

It is often convenient to simplify math problems mentally. There are several mental math techniques that are especially useful.

▬ Example 1 ▬

Use compensation to simplify.

a. 74×4

74 is close to 70.

$74 \times 4 = 70 \times 4$ (plus 4×4)

$\qquad = 280 + 16 = 296$

$74 \times 4 = 296$

b. $98 + 30$

98 is close to 100.

$98 + 30 = 100 + 30$ (minus 2)

$\qquad = 130 - 2 = 128$

$98 + 30 = 128$

Try It Use compensation to simplify.

a. 22×9 _____

b. 48×5 _____

c. $17 + 6$ _____

d. $33 - 5$ _____

e. 108×8 _____

f. $152 + 25$ _____

▬ Example 2 ▬

Use the Distributive Property to simplify 85×7.

Break 85 into $80 + 5$.
Multiply each piece by 7. Find 80×7 and 5×7.
Add the pieces together.

$85 \times 7 = (80 + 5) \times 7$
$\qquad = (80 \times 7) + (5 \times 7)$
$\qquad = (560) + (35)$
$\qquad = 595$

$85 \times 7 = (80 + 5) \times 7 = 595$

Try It Use the Distributive Property to simplify.

g. 56×8 _____

h. 4×104 _____

i. 5×45 _____

j. 9×42 _____

k. 7×64 _____

l. 3×55 _____

Estimating Sums and Differences

To estimate a sum or difference using *front-end estimation*, add or subtract using only the first digits of each number. Estimate the sum or difference of the remaining digits and add this to the first estimate.

When adding several numbers that are approximately equal, use *clustering* to estimate the sum. Replace all of the numbers with a single number close to them that is easy to multiply. Then multiply.

━━ Example 1 ━━

Estimate 640 + 521 using one-digit front-end estimation.

Step 1: Add the first digit in each number: 6 + 5 = 11.

Step 2: Add 60 because 40 + 21 is about 60.

640 + 521 is about 1160.

```
  640
+ 521
 1100
+  60
 1160
```

Try It Estimate 3785 − 1276 using front-end estimation.

  a. Which two digits will you subtract first? What is their difference? _____

  b. Estimate the difference of the remaining digits. _____

  c. Estimate 3785 − 1276. _____

Estimate using front-end estimation.

  d. 2118 + 4632 _____   **e.** 9380 − 5252 _____

━━ Example 2 ━━

Estimate 310 + 305 + 298 + 296 + 302 using clustering.

Each of the numbers is close to 300. There are 5 numbers.
300 + 300 + 300 + 300 + 300 = 5 × 300 = 1500

So, 310 + 305 + 298 + 296 + 302 is about 1500.

Try It Estimate 189 + 199 + 215 using clustering.

  f. What number is close to the three numbers being added? _____

  g. How many numbers are being added? _____

  h. Estimate 189 + 199 + 215. _____

Estimate using clustering.

  i. 468 + 525 + 491 + 501   **j.** 710 + 745 + 699 + 685 + 708

  _____   _____

Estimating Products and Quotients

Like sums and differences, products and quotients can be estimated when you don't need exact answers. To estimate a product or quotient using *rounding,* round all numbers so that each contains only one nonzero digit. Then multiply or divide.

To estimate using *compatible numbers,* rewrite the problem using numbers that go together easily. Then multiply or divide.

━━ Example 1 ━━

Estimate 87 × 104 using rounding.

$$\begin{array}{ccccc} 104 & \to & \text{Round 104 to 100.} & \to & 100 \\ \times\,87 & \to & \text{Round 87 to 90.} & \to & \times\,90 \\ & & & & \overline{9000} \end{array}$$

So, 87 × 104 is about 9000.

Try It Estimate 937 × 67 using rounding.

a. Round 937 to the nearest hundred. _____

b. Round 67 to the nearest ten. _____

c. Multiply the two rounded numbers to estimate 937 × 67. _____

Estimate, using rounding.

d. 280 × 32 _____   **e.** 77 × 21 _____   **f.** 86 × 402 _____

━━ Example 2 ━━

Estimate 154 ÷ 38 using compatible numbers.

Step 1: Decide which numbers go together easily.   Think: 154 is about **160**.
                                                            38 is about **40**.

Step 2: Substitute the compatible numbers   160 ÷ 40 = 4
        and find the quotient.

So, 154 ÷ 38 is about 4.

Try It

Estimate 472 ÷ 84 using compatible numbers.

g. Which two numbers go together easily? _____

h. Divide the compatible numbers to estimate 472 ÷ 84. _____

Estimate using compatible numbers.

i. 252 ÷ 61 _____   **j.** 536 ÷ 51 _____   **k.** 790 ÷ 92 _____

Order of Operations

To make sure everyone gets the same answer for any given problem, mathematicians use a set of rules known as the **order of operations.**

The rules for order of operations are:
1. Simplify inside parentheses.
2. Simplify exponents.
3. Multiply and divide from left to right.
4. Add and subtract from left to right.

▬ Example 1 ▬▬

Simplify $5 \times (2 + 4)$.

Follow the order of operations.

$$5 \times \mathbf{(2 + 4)}$$
$$\downarrow$$
$$= \mathbf{5} \times \quad \mathbf{6} = 30$$

Simplify inside parentheses first.

Multiply.

$5 \times (2 + 4)$ simplified is 30.

▬ Example 2 ▬▬

Simplify $8 \div 2^2$

$$8 \div \mathbf{2^2}$$
$$\downarrow$$
$$= 8 \div 4 = 2$$

Simplify exponents first.

Divide.

$8 \div 2^2$ simplified is 2.

Try It Simplify $6 + 4^2 - 12$. $\qquad 6 + \mathbf{4^2} - 12$

   a. There are no parentheses. So simplify exponents. $\qquad 6 +$ _____ $- 12$

   b. There are no numbers to multiply or divide. So add
   and subtract from left to right. Add the first two numbers. _____ $- 12$

   c. Subtract. _____

Simplify.

   d. $(35 - 15) \div 4$ _____

   e. $8 \times 2 + 4$ _____

   f. $17 - 5 \times 2$ _____

   g. $4 \times 6 \div 3$ _____

   h. $5 \times (5 + 6)$ _____

   i. $4^2 + 2 \div 2$ _____

   j. $10 \div 5 \times 2$ _____

   k. $5^2 - (3 \times 6)$ _____

   l. $3 \times 2^3 \div 6$ _____

   m. $8 + 5 - 6$ _____

Name _____

Numerical Patterns

A **numerical pattern** is a list of numbers that occur in some predictable way. Many patterns use addition and subtraction. To find the pattern, write the number that you need to add or subtract to find the next number in the pattern.

━━ Example 1 ━━

Find the next three numbers in this pattern: 25, 30, 35, 40,...

Step 1: Determine the pattern:

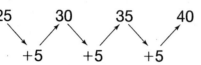

25   30   35   40

+5   +5   +5

Since each number in the pattern is 5 more than the number before, the pattern is add 5.

Step 2: Use the pattern to calculate the next three numbers.

40 + 5 = **45**   45 + 5 = **50**   50 + 5 = **55**

The next three numbers in the pattern are 45, 50, and 55.

Try It   Find the next three numbers in this pattern: 92, 90, 88, 86, ...

a. Pattern: _____   **b.** Next three numbers: _____

Find the next three numbers in the pattern.

c. 15, 30, 45, 60, ... _____   **d.** 24, 21, 18, 15, ... _____

━━ Example 2 ━━

Find the next three numbers in this pattern: 1, 7, 2, 8, 3, 9, 4,...

Step 1: Determine the pattern:

1   7   2   8   3   9   4

+6   −5   +6   −5   +6   −5

The pattern is add 6, subtract 5.

Step 2: Use the pattern to calculate the next three numbers.

4 + 6 = **10**   10 − 5 = **5**   5 + 6 = **11**

The next three numbers in the pattern are 10, 5, and 11.

Try It   Find the next three numbers in this pattern: 10, 20, 15, 25, 20, 30, ...

e. Pattern: _____   **f.** Next three numbers: _____

Find the next three numbers in the pattern.

g. 5, 4, 9, 8, 13, 12, ... _____   **h.** 6, 4, 8, 6, 10, 8, ... _____

i. 20, 22, 25, 27, 30, ... _____   **j.** 60, 50, 45, 35, 30, ... _____

Variables and Expressions

A **variable** is a quantity that can change or vary. Mathematicians use letters to represent variables.

A quantity that does not change is a **constant.**

An **expression** is a mathematical phrase involving constants, variables, and operation symbols. There are different ways to represent different operations. Four examples are shown below.

Addition:	$x + 6$	x is the variable.	6 is the constant.
Subtraction:	$91 - x$	x is the variable.	91 is the constant.
Multiplication:	$3x$ or $3 \times x$	x is the variable.	3 is the constant.
Division:	$12 \div x$ or $\frac{12}{x}$	x is the variable.	12 is the constant.

If you know the values of the variable, you can *evaluate* the expression by replacing the variable with each value. This is known as *substituting a value for the variable.*

━━ Example ━━

Evaluate $2x$ for $x = 4$, 6, and 8.

$2x$ means "2 times x." To evaluate the expression, you need to substitute a value for x.

When $x = 4$, substitute 4 for x: You can make a table to evaluate the expression for multiple values of x.

x	$2x$
4	$2 \times 4 = 8$
6	$2 \times 6 = 12$
8	$2 \times 8 = 16$

So $2x = 8$ when $x = 4$, $2x = 12$ when $x = 6$, and $2x = 16$ when $x = 8$.

Try It   Evaluate $x + 12$ for $x = 2$, 5, and 10.

a. Substitute 2 for x. Solve: $2 + 12 =$ _____

b. Substitute 5 for x. Solve: $5 + 12 =$ _____

c. Substitute 10 for x. Solve: $10 + 12 =$ _____

Evaluate each expression for $x = 2$, 5, and 10.

d. $6x$ _____ _____ _____

e. $x - 1$ _____ _____ _____

f. $50 \div x$ _____ _____ _____

g. $27 + x$ _____ _____ _____

h. $16 - x$ _____ _____ _____

i. $\frac{100}{x}$ _____ _____ _____

Name _____

Writing Expressions

Some words in English can be translated into specific
mathematical operations.

Word	Definition	Numerical Expression	Variable Expression
sum	The result of **adding** numbers	$7 + 2$	$8 + x$
difference	The result of **subtracting** numbers	$12 - 3$	$28 - y$
product	The result of **multiplying** numbers	4×16	$8c$
quotient	The result of **dividing** numbers	$81 \div 9$	$\frac{14}{s}$ or $14 \div s$

To translate situations that don't use these words, you need to choose
an operation that is appropriate for the situation. It may be easier to
choose an operation if you first replace the variable with a number.

━━ Example ━━

Write an expression to answer: What is the quotient of 99 divided by x?

Step 1: What operation is being done?   A quotient is the answer when dividing,
so use division to write the expression.

Step 2: Use the appropriate sign to
write the expression: $99 \div x$ or $\frac{99}{x}$

The expressions $99 \div x$ and $\frac{99}{x}$ shows the quotient of 99 divided by x.

Try It   Write an expression to answer: What is 12 minus r?

a. What operation is being done? _____.

b. Write the expression. _____

Write an expression to answer each question.

c. What is 32 times as big as y? _____

d. What is 24 more than n? _____

e. What is 11 less than b? _____

f. What is d divided by 5? _____

g. What is g plus 10? _____

h. Brian has p pencils and bought 4 more. How many does he have? _____

i. Tammy plants 6 rows of t tomato plants each.
How many tomato plants did she plant?   _____

Using Equations

An **equation** is a mathematical sentence that uses an equal sign, =, to show that two expressions are equal. An equation can be either true or false. For example, $13 + 12 = 25$ is true because both sides have the same value and $85 - 21 = 82$ is false because both sides of the equation do **not** have the same value.

An equation with a variable can also be true or false, depending on the value of the variable.

▬ Example ▬

Is the equation true for the given value of the variable?

a.　$4y = 24, y = 6$

　　$4 \times 6 \overset{?}{=} 24$　　　　Substitute 6 for y.

　　　$24 = 24$　　　　Multiply.

Since both sides of the equation have the same value, the equation is true.

b. $8 + a = 10, a = 3$

　　$8 + a \overset{?}{=} 10$　　　　Substitute 3 for a.

　　　$11 \neq 10$　　　　Add.

Since both sides of the equation do **not** have the same value, the equation is false.

Try It

Is the equation true for the given value of the variable: $28 \div x = 7, x = 4$?

a. What value will you substitute for x? _____

b. Rewrite the equation, substituting for x. _____

c. Is the equation you wrote in Item b true or false? _____

Is the equation true for the given value of the variable?

d. $k + 65 = 100, x = 25$ _____　　**e.** $9y = 72, y = 8$ _____

f. $56 - j = 40, j = 20$ _____　　**g.** $\frac{r}{3} = 5, r = 15$ _____

h. $2w = 60, w = 30$ _____　　**i.** $p - 6 = 6, p = 22$ _____

j. $7 \times b = 49, b = 7$ _____　　**k.** $m \div 4 = 2, m = 10$ _____

l. $40 + q = 60, q = 25$ _____　　**m.** $16 - h = 7, h = 9$ _____

Solving Equations

Sometimes you need to find the exact value that will make an equation true. This is known as *solving the equation*.

Think of equations as questions where the variable is read as "what number?" For example, $a + 3 = 10$ can be read as "What number plus 3 equals 10?" Use mental math to answer the question.

▬ Example ▬

Solve $y - 8 = 7$.

Step 1: Read as: "What number minus 8 equals 7?" $y - 8 = 7$

Step 2: Use mental math. $15 - 8 = 7$

Step 3: Check to see that the equation is true. $7 = 7$

In the equation $y - 8 = 7$, y is equal to 15.

Try It

Solve $a + 5 = 12$.

a. What number plus 5 equals 12? _____ so $a =$ _____

b. Show that the equation is true. _____

Solve $3x = 18$.

c. What number times 3 equals 18? _____ so $x =$ _____

d. Show that the equation is true. _____

Solve $m \div 3 = 20$.

e. What number divided by 3 = 20? _____ so $m =$ _____

f. Show that the equation is true. _____

Solve each equation.

g. $y + 15 = 50$ $y =$ _____   **h.** $b - 4 = 8$ $b =$ _____

i. $\frac{w}{2} = 6$ $w =$ _____   **j.** $3 \times c = 27$ $c =$ _____

k. $28 - p = 19$ $p =$ _____   **l.** $t + 8 = 26$ $t =$ _____

m. $11s = 110$ $s =$ _____   **n.** $81 \div k = 9$ $k =$ _____

o. $17 + r = 40$ $r =$ _____   **p.** $h \div 3 = 12$ $h =$ _____

Name _____

Decimal Notation

You can use what you know about place value to help you understand decimals. There are many ways to represent numbers. One way is to use a grid. A second way is to use numbers, and a third way is to use words. A place-value chart like the one at the right can help you understand decimals.

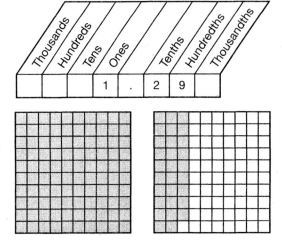

Grid form: ————————————————→

Number form: 1.29

Word form: one and twenty-nine hundredths

▬ Example 1 ▬

Write the decimal number represented by the grid.

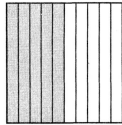

The grid is divided into 10 sections, so each section represents tenths. Five sections are shaded, so the grid represents 0.5.

Try It Write the decimal number represented by the grid.

a.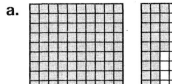

b.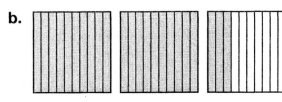

_____   _____

▬ Example 2 ▬

Write four and three hundred eleven thousandths as a decimal.

You know that the decimal point is read as "and", so the decimal is 4.311.

Try It Write each number as a decimal.

c. twelve hundredths _____   **d.** eight tenths _____

e. three and four hundred ninety-seven thousandths _____

f. five and twenty-six hundredths _____

g. six and forty-three hundredths _____

h. two and eight hundred seventy-four thousandths _____

Rounding Decimals

You can *round* numbers to estimate answers. To round a number,
look at the digit to the right of the place you want to round to. If the
digit is 5 or greater, round up. If it is less than 5, round down.

▬ Example 1 ▬

Round 34.0592 to the nearest hundredth.

Step 1: Find the place value.   The 5 is in the hundredths place.

Step 2: Look at the digit to the right   The digit is 9.

Step 3: If this digit is 5 or greater, round up.
If it's less than 5, round down.   9 is greater than 5, so round up.

Step 4: Drop the digits to the right.   The rounded number is 34.06.

34.0592 rounds to 34.06 when rounding to the nearest hundredth.

Try It Round 0.241 to the nearest tenth.

a. The tenths digit is _____. Underline it.

b. The digit to the right of the tenths digit is _____.

c. Is that digit 5 or greater? _____

d. Write the rounded number. Drop any digits to the right of tenths. _____

Round to the given place.

e. 4.652, tenths _____   **f.** 19.304, hundredths _____

▬ Example 2 ▬

What is the length of the eraser to the nearest
centimeter and the nearest tenth of a centimeter?

The end of the eraser is between the 5.5 mark
and the 6 mark. Use 5.7 as an estimate.

To the nearest centimeter, the eraser is 6.0 cm.
To the nearest tenth of a centimeter, it is 5.7 cm.

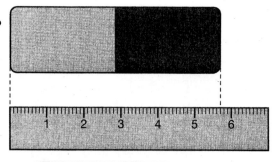

Try It Estimate the length of the paper clip
to the

g. nearest centimeter. _____

h. nearest tenth of a centimeter. _____

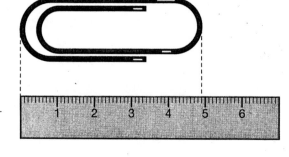

Name _____

Comparing and Ordering Decimals

To compare two decimals, write the decimals so that the decimals have the same number of digits after the decimal point. Remember: writing or *annexing* zeros to the right of a decimal does not change its value.

▬ Example 1 ▬

Use > or < to compare 0.08 and 0.6.

Step 1: Annex a zero to 0.6 so that both decimals have   0.08
the same number of digits after the decimal point.

Step 2: Compare place values starting with the digit at the left.   0.60
The ones digits are the same. Compare the tenths digits.

Since 0 is less than 6, 0.08 < 0.6.

Try It Use > or < to compare 3.409 and 3.48.

  a. How many digits are after the decimal point in 3.409? _____

  b. Rewrite 3.48 with the same number of digits after the decimal point. _____

  c. Compare, starting with the ones digits. 3.409 _____ 3.48

Use > or < to compare each pair of numbers.

  d. 2.33 _____ 2.033   **e.** 41.039 _____ 41.05   **f.** 0.479 _____ 0.45

▬ Example 2 ▬

Order from least to greatest: 0.72, 0.227, 1.07.

Write the numbers so that each has the same number   0.72 = 0.720
of decimal places.   0.227 = 0.227
                                                           1.07 = 1.070
Then compare the numbers starting with the digits on the left.   1 > 0
                                                                  7 > 2

The numbers from least to greatest are 0.227, 0.72, 1.07.

Try It Order from least to greatest.

  g. 3.04, 0.304, 0.34 _____

  h. 0.205, 0.6, 0.46 _____

  i. 0.98, 0.908, 0.098 _____

  j. 23.04, 32.40, 32.04 _____

  k. 11.011, 10.101, 10.011 _____

Scientific Notation

Scientific notation is an easier way to write very large and very small numbers. A number in scientific notation is written as the product of a number between 1 and 10 and a power of 10. You write the power of 10 using exponents, with 10 as the base and the number of times 10 is a factor as the exponent.

━━ Example 1 ━━

Write 4.2×10^7 in standard form.

The power of 10 tells you how many places to move the decimal point. Move the decimal point <u>to the right</u> 7 places.

$4.2 \times 10^7 = 42,000,000$

7 places

So, $4.2 \times 10^7 = 42,000,000$.

Try It Write 6.12×10^9 in standard form.

a. How many places to the *right* will the decimal point move? _____

b. $6.12 \times 10^9 =$ _____

Write each number in standard form.

c. 5.6×10^7 _____

d. 1.82×10^6 _____

━━ Example 2 ━━

Write 7,089,000 in scientific notation.

Write 7,089,000 as a product of two numbers. The first factor is the decimal number with one digit before the decimal. To write this number, move the decimal point <u>to the left</u> 6 places.

7,089,000

6 places

The second factor is a power of 10. The exponent is the number of places the decimal point was moved.

10^6

So, $7,089,000 = 7.089 \times 10^6$

Try It Write 908,000 in scientific notation.

e. How many places to the *left* will the decimal point move? _____

f. What is the first factor? _____

g. What is the second factor? _____

h. $908,000 =$ _____

Write each number in scientific notation.

i. 423,000,000 _____

j. 50,600,000 _____

k. 120,000, _____

l. 90,060,000,000 _____

Estimating with Decimals

Two ways to estimate with decimals are *rounding* and *compatible numbers*. Compatible numbers often work better for estimating products and quotients.

━━ Example 1 ━━

Use rounding to estimate the sum: $12.89 + $14.29.

Round each number to the nearest dollar by looking at the first number to the right of the decimal point.

$$\begin{array}{ccc} \$12.89 & \rightarrow & \$13.00 \\ +\ 14.29 & \rightarrow & +\ 14.00 \end{array}$$

Add. $27.00

The estimated sum is $27.00.

Try It Use rounding to estimate the difference: 124.772 − 49.55.

a. Round to the nearest whole number.   124.777 _____   49.55 _____

b. Subtract to estimate the difference. _____

Use rounding to estimate each sum or difference.

c. $23.78 + $79.82 _____   **d.** 72.089 + 11.78 _____

e. $54.88 − $23.40 _____   **f.** 188.36 − 59.99 _____

━━ Example 2 ━━

Use compatible numbers to estimate 239.15 ÷ 33.7.

Look for numbers that are close to those being divided but are easy to divide mentally.

$$\begin{array}{cc} 239.15 & \div\ 33.7 \\ \downarrow & \downarrow \end{array}$$

Divide.   240 ÷ 30 = 8

The estimated quotient is 8.

Try It Use compatible numbers to estimate 88.23 × 91.009.

g. Which two numbers are easier to multiply? _____

h. Multiply the compatible numbers to estimate 88.23 × 91.009. _____

Use compatible numbers to estimate each product or quotient.

i. 48.23 × 5.45 _____   **j.** 74.87 × 8.75 _____

k. 65.04 ÷ 7.83 _____   **l.** 129.49 ÷ 11.24 _____

m. 37.8 × 8.9 _____   **n.** 519.9 ÷ 90.6 _____

Adding and Subtracting Decimal Numbers

When you add or subtract decimals, first line up the decimal points, and annex zeros if necessary. Then add or subtract as if you were adding or subtracting whole numbers.

▬ Example 1 ▬

Add 1.4 and 1.63. Use models if you like.

Line up the decimal points.
Annex zeros so that both numbers have the same number of digits to the right of the decimal point.

$$\begin{array}{r} 1.4\mathbf{0} \\ +\ 1.63 \\ \hline 3.03 \end{array}$$

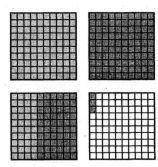

Add, beginning with the hundredths.   3.03

The sum of 1.4 and 1.63 is 3.03.

Try It Add. Use models if you like.

a. $\begin{array}{r} 0.59 \\ +\ 0.6 \\ \hline \end{array}$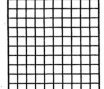

b. $\begin{array}{r} 1.2 \\ +\ 0.23 \\ \hline \end{array}$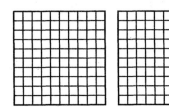

c. 2.026 + 0.42 _____

d. 0.713 + 6.8 _____

▬ Example 2 ▬

Subtract 1.7 − 0.34. Use models if you like.

Line up the decimal points.
Annex zeros so that both numbers have the same number of digits to the right of the decimal point.

$$\begin{array}{r} 1.7\mathbf{0} \\ -\ 0.34 \\ \hline 1.36 \end{array}$$

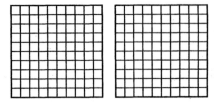

Subtract, beginning with the hundredths.   1.36

The difference between 1.7 and 0.34 is 1.36.

Try It Subtract. Use models if you like.

e. $\begin{array}{r} 1.06 \\ -\ 0.8 \\ \hline \end{array}$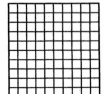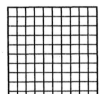

f. $\begin{array}{r} 1.9 \\ -\ 1.49 \\ \hline \end{array}$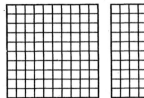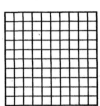

g. 72 − 13.409 _____

h. 32.4 − 0.481 _____

Solving Decimal Equations: Addition and Subtraction

You can solve addition and subtraction equations involving decimals by using mental math. You can also work backward to solve for the variable.

▬▬ Example ▬▬▬▬

Solve $x + 5.3 = 6.6$.

Step 1: Think: What number plus 5.3 equals 6.6? $x + 5.3 = 6.6$

Step 2: Use mental math. $\mathbf{1.3} + 5.3 = 6.6$

Step 3: Check to see that the equation is true. $6.6 = 6.6$ ✓

You could also work backward to solve for x.

When you work backward, you start with the answer. To get to the beginning, you can subtract the known addend. This will give you the same answer. $6.6 - 5.3 = 1.3$

In the equation $x + 5.3 = 6.6$, x is equal to 1.3.

Try It   Solve $a - 5.2 = 3.1$.

a. What number minus 5.2 equals 3.1? _____ so $a =$ _____

b. Show that the equation is true. _____

Solve $0.5 + b = 2.3$.

c. What number plus 0.5 equals 2.3? _____ so $b =$ _____

d. Show that the equation is true. _____

Solve $8.6 - c = 4.3$.

e. What number subtracted from 8.6 equals 4.3? _____ so $c =$ _____

f. Show that the equation is true. _____

Solve.

g. $d + 1.8 = 2.9$ _____   **h.** $2.9 + e = 3.5$ _____

i. $\$1.95 + f = \$2.15$ _____   **j.** $g + \$0.75 = \$1.00$ _____

k. $h - 2.4 = 2.1$ _____   **l.** $0.35 - j = 0.25$ _____

m. $k - 0.12 = 0.24$ _____   **n.** $0.45 - y = 0.44$ _____

Name _____

Multiplying a Whole Number by a Decimal

When you multiply a whole number by a decimal, multiply as though you were multiplying two whole numbers. Then count the number of digits after the decimal in the factors. Write the answer with the same number of decimal places after the decimal point.

▬ Example ▬

Multiply 0.45×3.

One way to find a product is to use repeated addition.

A second way to find the product is to multiply as though you were multiplying two whole numbers.

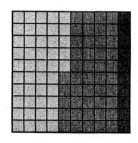 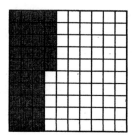

Count the number of digits after the decimal point in each factor. There are two digits after the decimal point in 0.45. There are no digits after the decimal point in 3.

Multiply.

Place the decimal point. Since the two factors have a total of two digits after the decimal point, the product will also have two digits after the decimal point.

So, $0.45 \times 3 = 01.35$.

$0.45 \leftarrow$ 2 decimal places

$\underline{\times\ 3} \leftarrow$ 0 decimal places

$1.35 \leftarrow$ 2 decimal places

Try It Multiply 12.79×5.

a. The decimal factor is _____.

b. How many decimal places will be in the answer? _____

c. What is the product? _____

Multiply.

d. 32.4×6 _____

e. 5.6×4 _____

f. 324×0.28 _____

g. 25.98×12 _____

h. 1.65×10 _____

i. 1.11×34 _____

j. 25×5.7 _____

k. 8.111×9 _____

l. 18×1.41 _____

m. 6×3.422 _____

n. 1.02×6 _____

o. 9×20.4 _____

Multiplying a Decimal by a Decimal

Multiply a decimal by a decimal as if the two numbers were whole numbers. Then count the number of digits to the right of the decimal point in each decimal factor. Finally, write the product. The product should have the same number of digits to the right of the decimal as there are in both factors. In some cases, you must annex zeros in order to have the correct number of digits to the right of the decimal point.

▬ Example ▬▬▬

Multiply: 0.31×0.18.

Count the number of digits after the decimal point in each factor. There are two digits after the decimal point in 0.31. There are two digits after the decimal point in 0.18.

Multiply.

Place the decimal point. The two factors have a total of four digits after the decimal point, so the product will also have four digits after the decimal point. Since there are only 3 digits in the product, you will need to **annex** one zero. Notice that another zero is placed before the decimal point.

$$
\begin{array}{r}
0.31 \leftarrow 2 \text{ decimal places} \\
\times\, 0.18 \leftarrow 2 \text{ decimal places} \\
\hline
248 \\
31 \\
\hline
0.0558 \leftarrow 4 \text{ decimal places}
\end{array}
$$

So, $0.31 \times 0.18 = 0.0558$.

Try It Multiply: 2.08×0.4.

  a. How many decimal places are in 2.08? _____

  b. How many decimal places are in 0.4? _____

  c. How many decimal places will be in the product? _____

  d. What is the product? _____

Multiply.

e. 0.28 $\times$ 3.2	**f.** 0.183 $\times$ 2.4	**g.** 15.21 $\times$ 0.45	**h.** 5.07 $\times$ 0.73
_____	_____	_____	_____

i. 8.4×0.01 _____

j. 1.4×0.001 _____

k. 0.94×0.001 _____

l. 0.001×0.001 _____

m. 300×0.002 _____

n. 0.005×200 _____

Dividing by a Whole Number

When you divide a decimal by a whole number, divide the decimal as if you were dividing whole numbers. Then place the decimal point in the quotient directly above the decimal point in the dividend. Sometimes you may need to annex zeros in the dividend so that you can divide until the remainder is zero.

```
  0.24 ←quotient
5)1.2
  ↗    ↖
divisor  dividend
```

Example

Divide: 435 ÷ 50.

Divide 50 into 435. Write the quotient above the 5.

Find 8 × 50 = 400. Subtract from 435.

Write a 0 after the decimal point in 435.

Divide 350 by 50. Write the quotient above the 0.

Write the decimal point in the quotient above the decimal point in the dividend.

So, 435 ÷ 50 = 8.7

```
      8.7
50)435.0
   400
    35 0
    35 0
```

Try It   Divide 83.2 ÷ 4.

a. Divide as if you were dividing whole numbers. Show your work.

$4\overline{)83.2}$

b. Will you need to annex zeros in the dividend? _____

c. Write the quotient. Place the decimal point above the decimal point in the quotient.

Divide. Write your answer above the dividend.

d. $3\overline{)22.65}$ e. $5\overline{)376.15}$ f. $7\overline{)91.14}$ g. $12\overline{)2.172}$

h. $6\overline{)42.9}$ i. $4\overline{)1.04}$ j. $8\overline{)50.2}$ k. $25\overline{)114.9}$

Dividing by a Decimal

When you divide by a decimal, you need to rewrite the problem so that you are dividing by a whole number. You can do this by multiplying the divisor by a power of 10 that will make the divisor a whole number and multiplying the dividend by the same power of 10. Remember that you can multiply a decimal by 10, 100, or 1000 by moving the decimal point to the right 1, 2, or 3 places.

$$20. \leftarrow \text{quotient}$$
$$1.2\overline{)24.0}$$
$$\text{divisor} \quad \text{dividend}$$

▬ Example ▬

Find the quotient: $7.84 \div 1.4$.

Multiply the divisor and the dividend by 10 to make the divisor a whole number. Move the decimal point 1 place to the right in each number.

$$1.4\overline{)7.84} \quad \rightarrow \quad 14.\overline{)78.4}$$

Divide as you would with whole numbers.

$$\begin{array}{r} 5.6 \\ 14.\overline{)78.4} \\ \underline{70} \\ 8\,4 \\ \underline{8\,4} \end{array}$$

Remember to write the decimal point in the quotient above the moved decimal point in the dividend.

So, $7.84 \div 1.4 = 5.6$.

Try It Divide: $5.65 \div 4.52$.

a. Divide as if you were dividing whole numbers. Show your work.

$$4.52\overline{)5.65}$$

b. How many decimal places are in the divisor? _____

c. Move the decimal point in the divisor and dividend. Will you need to annex zeros in the dividend? _____

d. Write the quotient. Place the decimal point above the moved decimal point in the quotient.

Divide. Write your answer above the dividend.

e. $0.04\overline{)0.38}$ f. $0.25\overline{)4.05}$ g. $0.85\overline{)7.055}$ h. $3.7\overline{)0.296}$

i. $5.6 \div 0.4$ _____ j. $0.72 \div 0.9$ _____

k. $2.25 \div 0.5$ _____ l. $0.636 \div 0.6$ _____

m. $2.52 \div 0.7$ _____ n. $0.027 \div 0.03$ _____

Solving Decimal Equations:
Multiplication and Division

You can solve multiplication and division equations using mental math and number sense. Use mental math to determine the digits in the answer and number sense to decide where to place the decimal point.

━━ **Example** ━━━━

Solve $4x = 3.6$.

Step 1: Think of the numbers as whole numbers. $4x = 3.6 \rightarrow 4x = 36$

Step 2: Think: What number times 4 equals 36? $4x = 36$

Step 3: Use mental math. $4 \times 9 = 36$

Step 4: Determine where to place the decimal point.
There is one decimal place in the product, 3.6,
so there should be one decimal place in one of
the factors. Since there is not a decimal place
in the known factor, 4, there will be one decimal
place in the value of x. So $x = 0.9$.

Step 5: Check to see that the equation is true. $4 \times 0.9 = 3.6$

In the equation $4x = 3.6$, x is equal to 0.9.

Try It   Solve $a \div 6 = 0.04$.

a. Rewrite the equation using whole numbers. _____

b. What number divided by 6 equals 4? _____

c. The divisor, 6, is a whole number and there are
two digits after the decimal point in the quotient, 0.04.
How many digits are after the decimal point in the dividend, a? _____

d. $a = $ _____

e. Show that the equation is true. _____

Solve each equation.

f. $2r = 1.4$ $r = $ _____   **g.** $s \div 4 = 2.2$ $s = $ _____

h. $\dfrac{b}{5} = 0.5$ $b = $ _____   **i.** $0.7c = 0.49$ $c = $ _____

j. $1.5d = 0.45$ $d = $ _____   **k.** $n \div 3 = 1.2$ $n = $ _____

l. $0.09c = 0.108$ $c = $ _____   **m.** $\dfrac{g}{2} = 3.4$ $g = $ _____

verting in the Metric System

tric system is a system of measurements used to describe
g, how heavy, or how big something is. The metric system
efixes to describe amounts that are much larger or smaller
e base unit. The base units for measuring length, mass, and
are shown in the table below. The prefixes used most often are
eaning 1000; **centi-,** meaning $\frac{1}{100}$; and **milli-,** meaning $\frac{1}{1000}$.

rert a unit in the metric system, you need to multiply or divide
wer of 10. The table below lists the powers of 10 to use when
ing. When converting to a larger unit, your answer gets smaller.
onverting to a smaller unit, your answer gets larger. For
e, if you are given a distance in millimeters, it will take fewer
ters to equal that same distance.

÷ 1000	÷ 100	÷ 10	base unit	× 10	× 100	× 1000
kilo-	hecto-	deca-	meter gram liter	deci-	centi-	milli-
× 1000	× 100	× 10	base unit	÷ 10	÷ 100	÷ 1000

xample

t 34,000 milliliters to liters.

converting from a smaller unit to a larger unit, so you
de. Refer to the conversion table to find the divisor.
onverting from milliliters to liters, divide by 1000. $34,000 \div 1,000 = 34$

000 milliliters = 34 liters.

Convert.

grams = ? milligrams

you converting from a smaller unit
a larger unit or a larger unit to a smaller unit? _____

you multiply or divide? _____

at number will you multiply or divide by? _____

grams = _____ milligrams

eters = _____ centimeters   **c.** 162 kilograms = _____ grams

00 milliliters = _____ liters   **e.** 25,000 millimeters = _____ meters

Perimeter

The distance around the outside of a figure is known as the **perimeter.** To find the perimeter of a given geometric figure, you add the lengths of the sides.

━━ Example 1 ━━

Find the perimeter.

Add the lengths of the four sides.

$6 + 8 + 6 + 8 = 28$

The perimeter is 28 inches.

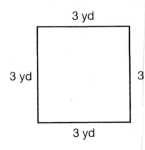

Try It Find each perimeter by adding the lengths of the sides.

a.

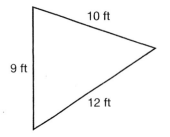

_____

b.

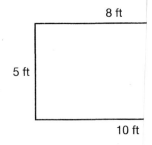

━━ Example 2 ━━

Find the length of the unknown side.

In a rectangle, opposite sides are equal. Suppose you extend the sides of the figure to make a 5 ft by 10 ft rectangle. Then the left side and right side are both 5 ft. You know part of the right side is 3 ft. Therefore, the unknown length is 2 ft.

Try It Find the length of each unknown side.

c.

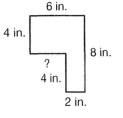

In a rectangle, opposite sides ar...

_____ – _____ = _____

The unknown side is _____ .

d.

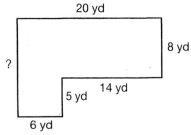

_____

e.

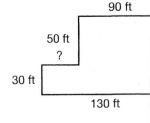

Cor...

You...
will...
Whe...

So, ...

Try

a.

b. 6...

d. 4...

Name _____

Using Conversion Factors

The customary system is another system of measurement. It is not based on powers of 10. In order to convert from one unit to another, you need to know the **conversion factor,** or the number of units that another unit is equal to.

Length	Weight	Liquid Capacity
1 foot (ft) = 12 inches (in.) 1 yard (yd) = 3 feet (ft) 1 mile (mi) = 5280 feet (ft)	1 pound (lb) = 16 ounces (oz)	1 gallon (gal) = 4 quarts (qt)

To convert from a larger unit to a smaller unit, you *multiply* by the appropriate conversion factor. To convert from a smaller unit to a larger unit, you *divide* by the appropriate conversion factor.

Example

How many feet are in 3 yards? In 24 inches?

When you convert from a larger unit (yard) to a smaller unit (foot), multiply the number of yards by the number of feet in a yard.

1 yard = 3 feet
3 × 3 = 9

There are 9 feet in 3 yards.

When you convert from a smaller unit (inches) to a larger unit (feet), divide the number of feet by the number of inches in a foot.

1 foot = 12 inches
24 ÷ 12 = 2

There are 2 feet in 24 inches.

Try It Convert.

a. 48 ounces = ? pounds

Are you converting from a smaller unit to a larger unit or a larger unit to a smaller unit? _____

Will you multiply or divide? _____

What number will you multiply or divide by? _____

48 ounces = _____ pounds

b. 16 quarts = _____ gallons

c. 10 miles = _____ feet

d. 5 feet = _____ inches

e. 100 pounds = _____ ounces

f. 10,560 feet = _____ miles

g. 16 gallons = _____ quarts

Area of Squares and Rectangles

The **area** of a figure is the amount of surface it covers. Area is usually measured by the number of unit squares of the same size that fit into the figure. If a figure is labeled with inches, then the area is expressed in **square inches (in²)**. A square inch is a square whose sides measure one inch. A **square centimeter (cm²)** is a square whose sides measure one centimeter.

The **base** of a square or rectangle is the distance across the bottom. The **height** is the distance up a side. The area of any square or rectangle is equal to the base times the height.

━━ Example ━━

Find the area of the rectangle.

Each side is measured in centimeters, so the area will be measured in square centimeters (cm²).

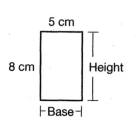

Find the area by multiplying base and height.

$5 \text{ cm} \times 8 \text{ cm} = 40 \text{ cm}^2$

The area of the rectangle is 40 square centimeters.

Try It Find the area of each rectangle.

a.

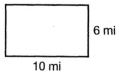

What is the base? _____

What is the height? _____

Multiply base and height to find the area. _____

b.  _____

c. _____

d. 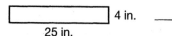 _____

e. _____

f. 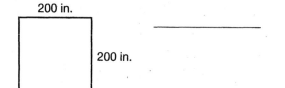 _____

g. 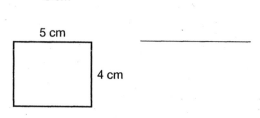 _____

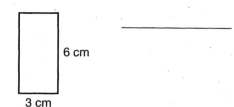

Area of Parallelograms

A **parallelogram** is a four-sided figure whose opposite sides are parallel. A parallelogram has the same area as a rectangle of equal base and height.

To find the area of a parallelogram, use the same formula as that for the area of a rectangle: base × height = area. The height of a parallelogram is always a vertical measure from the base, not a slanted measure. Area is always represented in square units.

▬ Example ▬

Find the area of the parallelogram.

Use the formula base × height = area.
The base of the parallelogram is 12 cm.
The height of the parallelogram is 6 cm.

The area of the parallelogram is 72 cm².

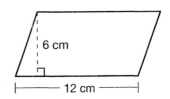

12 cm × 6 cm = 72 cm²

Try It Find each area. Remember to write each area in square units.

a.

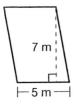

The base is _____.

The height is _____.

Multiply. The area is _____.

b.

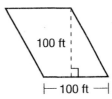

The base is _____.

The height is _____.

Multiply. The area is _____.

c. 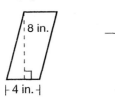 _____

d. 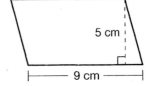 _____

e.  _____

f. 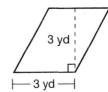 _____

g. _____

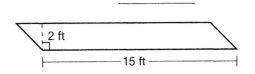

h. 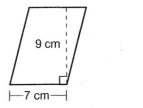 _____

Name  _____

Area of Triangles

The area of a triangle equals half the area of a rectangle whose base and height are the same as the triangle's. You can find the area of a triangle by calculating the area of the rectangle that surrounds it and dividing that in half. You can also use the area formula for a triangle.

▬ Example ▬

Find the area of this triangle.

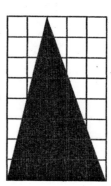

Method One: The area of the rectangular grid is 5 × 8, or 40 square units. Since the triangle on the grid covers only half of the squares, the area of the triangle is half of 40, or 20 square units.

Method Two: Use the formula base × height ÷ 2 = area. The base of the triangle is 5 units. The height of the triangle is 8 units.

$5 \times 8 \div 2 = 20$

The area of the triangle is 20 square units.

Try It   Find each area.

a.

Base _____   Height _____

_____ × _____ ÷ 2 = _____

Area _____

b.

7 ft

10 ft

Base _____   Height _____

_____ × _____ ÷ 2 = _____

Area _____

c.

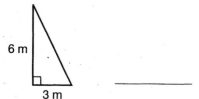

6 m

3 m

_____

d.

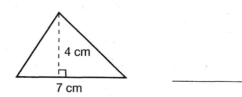

4 cm

7 cm

_____

e.

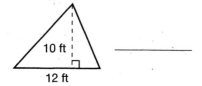

10 ft

12 ft

_____

f.

8 cm

4 cm

_____

40

Discovering Pi

The **radius** of a circle is any segment from
the center to any point on the circle. The
diameter of a circle is any segment from
one point on the circle to another point on
the circle, that passes through the center.

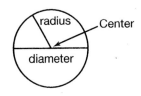

The **circumference** of a circle is the distance around the circle. For
any circle, the circumference divided by the diameter always equals
3.14159265.... This value is called **pi** and is represented by the
Greek letter π. If you know the diameter, you can use π to find the
circumference. 3.14 is used as an approximation for π.

Diameter × π = circumference

━━ Example 1 ━━

Find the diameter of this circle.

The diameter is equal to 2 times the radius.
The radius of this circle is 6 inches.

The diameter is 12 inches.

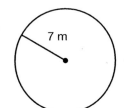

6 in.

$2 \times 6 = 12$

Try It Find the diameter of each circle.

a.

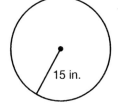

15 in.

b.

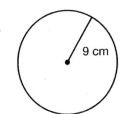

7 m

c.

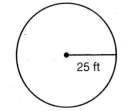

9 cm

d.

25 ft

━━ Example 2 ━━

Find the circumference of this circle. Use 3.14 for π.

Use the formula diameter × π = circumference.
Substitute 8 for the diameter and 3.14 for π.

The circumference is 25.12 m.

8 m

$8 \times 3.14 = 25.12$

Try It Find the circumference of each circle. Use 3.14 for π.

e.

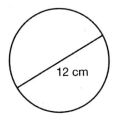

12 cm

f.

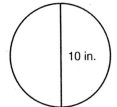

10 in.

g.

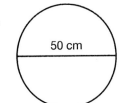

50 cm

h.

15 m

© Scott Foresman Addison Wesley 6

Area of Circles

The circumference and the diameter of a circle are related by the number π. The radius and the area of a circle are also related by the number π. If you know the radius of a circle, you can use π to find the area.

Area = π × r^2, where r is the radius.

━━ Example 1 ━━

Find the radius of this circle.

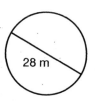

The radius is one half of the diameter of a circle.
The radius of this circle is 14 m.

The radius is 14 m.

$\frac{28}{2} = 14$

Try It Find the radius of each circle.

a.

b.

c.

d.

_____   _____

━━ Example 2 ━━

Find the area of this circle. Use 3.14 for π.

Use the formula area = π × r^2.
Substitute 10 for r, the radius, and 3.14 for π.

The area is 314 square meters, or 314 m^2.

$3.14 × 10^2 = 3.14 × 100 = 314$

Try It Find the area of each circle. Use 3.14 for π.

e.

f.

g.

h.

_____   _____   _____   _____

i.

j.

k.

l.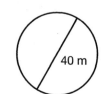

_____   _____   _____   _____

Area of Irregular Figures

Figures are not always perfect rectangles, triangles or circles. To find the area of an irregular figure, you may need to break it down into smaller familiar figures, and then find the area of each smaller figure.

▬ Example ▬

Find the area of this figure.

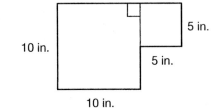

Step 1: Identify the smaller figures that make up the larger figure. The figure is made up of two squares.

Step 2: Find the area of each of the smaller figures. The area of a square is base times height.

The base and height of the larger square are 10 in. Substitute the values in the formula: 10×10. The area of the larger square is 100 in^2.

The base and height of the smaller square are 5 in. Substitute the values in the formula: 5×5. The area of the smaller square is 25 in^2.

Step 3: Decide how the figures make up the larger figure. Add the areas of the smaller figures to find the area of the larger figure.

$100 + 25 = 125$

So, the area of the figure is 125 in^2.

Try It Find the area of each figure.

a. Identify the figures in the drawing.

_____

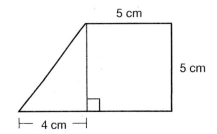

Find the area of one figure. _____

Find the area of the other figure. _____

Add both areas. _____ + _____ = _____

The area of the figure is _____.

b.
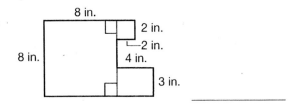

c.
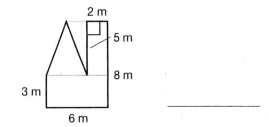

Divisibility

A whole number is **divisible** by another whole number if the first number can be divided by the second number without leaving a remainder. Twelve is divisible by two since $12 \div 2 = 6$. Twelve is not divisible by five since $12 \div 5 = 2$ R2.

━━ Example 1 ━━

Is 35 divisible by 2, 5, and 10? To decide if a whole number is divisible by 2, 5, or 10, you can start at zero and count by 2s, 5s, or 10s. You can also use divisibility rules.

If the ones digit is even, the number is divisible by 2.
If the ones digit is 0 or 5, the number is divisible by 5.
If the ones digit is 0, the number is divisible by 10.

The ones digit is 5, so 35 is divisible by 5. It is not divisible by 2 or 10.

Try It Tell whether the number is divisible by 2, 5, or 10. Use the rules above.

a. 40   What is the ones digit? _____

Is the number divisible by 2? _____   By 5? _____   By 10? _____

40 is divisible by _____.

b. 85 _____   **c.** 50 _____   **d.** 136 _____

━━ Example 2 ━━

Is 108 divisible by 3 and 9? To decide if a whole number is divisible by 3 or 9, you can count by 3s, or 9s. You can also use divisibility rules.

If the sum of the digits is divisible by 3, the number is divisible by 3.
If the sum of the digits is divisible by 9, the number is divisible by 9.

The sum of the digits in 108 is $1 + 0 + 8 = 9$. Since 9 is divisible by both 3 and 9, 108 is divisible by both 3 and 9.

Try It Tell whether the number is divisible by 3 or 9. Use the rules above.

e. 342   Find the sum of the digits. _____

Is the sum divisible by 3? _____   By 9? _____

342 is divisible by _____.

f. 255 _____   **g.** 204 _____   **h.** 441 _____

Prime Factorization

Every whole number greater than 1 is either a **prime number** or a **composite number**. A prime number has exactly two factors: 1 and itself. A composite number has more than two factors. The numbers 0 and 1 are neither prime nor composite.

▬ Example 1 ▬

The factors of 185 are 1, 5, 37, and 185.
Is 185 a prime number or a composite number?

Since there are more than two factors of 185, the number is a composite number.

Try It Given the number and its factors, tell whether it is prime or composite.

a. 25: 1, 5, 25 _____

b. 83: 1, 83 _____

c. 54: 1, 2, 3, 6, 9, 18, 27, 54 _____

d. 68: 1, 2, 4, 17, 34, 68 _____

▬ Example 2 ▬

Write the prime factorization of 50. Tell whether it is prime or composite.

To decide if a number is prime or composite, you need to find the factors. You can use a factor tree to find the prime factors. If the prime factorization is 1 × the number, the number is a prime number. If the prime factorization is **not** 1 × the number, the number is a composite number.

Here are two factor trees that show the prime factors of 50.

You get the same prime factors each way.

$50 = 2 \times 5 \times 5 \leftarrow$ Prime Factorization

Since the prime factorization is **not** 1 × the number, 50 is a composite number.

Try It Write the prime factorization of each number. Then tell whether the number is prime or composite.

e. 18 = _____

f. 23 = _____

g. 27 = _____

h. 60 = _____

i. 93 = _____

j. 115 = _____

Least Common Multiples

A **multiple** of a number is the product of the number and a whole
number. When the same number is a multiple of two or more numbers,
it is a **common multiple**. The smallest common multiple of two
numbers is the **least common multiple (LCM)**.

▬ Example ▬▬▬

Find the least common multiple (LCM) of 15 and 20.

List the common multiples of 15 and 20.

Multiples of 15:	15	30	45	**60**	...
	1 × 15	2 × 15	3 × 15	4 × 15	

Multiples of 20:	20	40	**60**	80	...
	1 × 20	2 × 20	3 × 20	4 × 20	

The LCM is the smallest number that appears on both lists. The LCM
of 15 and 20 is 60.

Try It Find the least common multiple (LCM) of each pair
of numbers.

a. 6 and 9   Multiples of 6:   6,   12,   18,   24,   30   LCM: _____

Multiples of 9:   9,   18,   27,   36,   45

b. 12 and 18   Multiples of 12:   12,   24,   36,   48,   60   LCM _____

Multiples of 18:   18,   36,   54,   72,   90

Find the least common multiple (LCM) of 8 and 10.

c. Write the first five multiples of each number.

Multiples of 8: _____

Multiples of 10: _____

d. Choose the smallest number that appears on both lists. _____

Find the least common multiple (LCM) of each pair of numbers.

e. 5, 7   **f.** 4, 6

Multiples of 5: _____   Multiples of 4: _____

Multiples of 7: _____   Multiples of 6: _____

LCM: _____   LCM: _____

Name _____

Understanding Fractions

A **fraction** describes part of a whole when the whole is cut into equal pieces. The **numerator**, or top number, tells how many parts are named. The **denominator**, or bottom number, gives the number of parts in the whole.

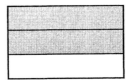

$\dfrac{2}{3}$ ← numerator
← denominator

━━ Example ━━

What fraction does the shaded part represent?

Find the numerator by counting the number of shaded parts. There are 5 shaded parts so the numerator is 5.

Find the denominator by counting the total number of parts in the whole. There are 6 parts in the whole so the denominator is 6.

The fraction is $\dfrac{5}{6}$.

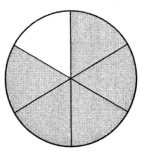

Try It What fraction does the shaded part represent?

a.

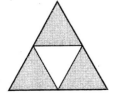

1. Count the shaded parts. What is the numerator? _____

2. Count the total number of parts. What is the denominator? _____

3. Write the fraction. _____

b.

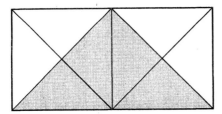

_____

c.

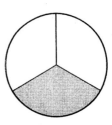

_____

d.

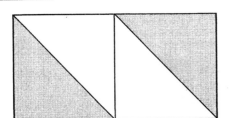

_____

e.

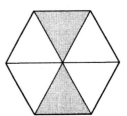

_____

Fractions in Lowest Terms

Equivalent fractions are two fractions that name the same amount. You can find equivalent fractions by multiplying or dividing the numerator and the denominator by the same nonzero number. This is the same as multiplying or dividing the fraction by 1.

── Example 1 ──

Find two fractions that are equivalent to $\frac{5}{10}$.

Numerator ⟶ $\frac{5 \times 2}{10 \times 2} = \frac{10}{20}$ $\frac{5}{10}$ is equivalent to $\frac{10}{20}$.
Denominator ⟶

Numerator ⟶ $\frac{5 \div 5}{10 \div 5} = \frac{1}{2}$ $\frac{5}{10}$ is equivalent to $\frac{1}{2}$.
Denominator ⟶

The fractions $\frac{5}{10}$, $\frac{10}{20}$, and $\frac{1}{2}$ are equivalent.

Try It Multiply to find an equivalent fraction.

a. $\frac{2}{6} = \frac{2 \times \square}{6 \times \square} = \frac{\square}{\square}$

b. $\frac{4}{5} = \frac{4 \times \square}{5 \times \square} = \frac{\square}{\square}$

Divide to find an equivalent fraction.

c. $\frac{6}{8} = \frac{6 \div \square}{8 \div \square} = \frac{\square}{\square}$

d. $\frac{3}{12} = \frac{3 \div \square}{12 \div \square} = \frac{\square}{\square}$

── Example 2 ──

A fraction is in **lowest terms** when no whole number can be divided evenly into both the numerator and the denominator. A fraction in lowest terms is equivalent to the original fraction.

Write $\frac{8}{24}$ in lowest terms.

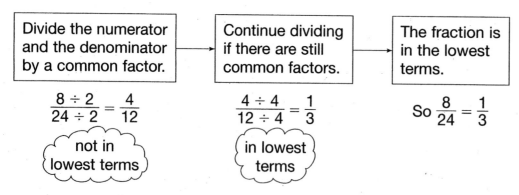

| Divide the numerator and the denominator by a common factor. | Continue dividing if there are still common factors. | The fraction is in the lowest terms. |

$\frac{8 \div 2}{24 \div 2} = \frac{4}{12}$ $\frac{4 \div 4}{12 \div 4} = \frac{1}{3}$ So $\frac{8}{24} = \frac{1}{3}$

(not in lowest terms)   (in lowest terms)

Try It Write each fraction in lowest terms.

e. $\frac{4}{10}$ _____

f. $\frac{15}{60}$ _____

g. $\frac{8}{28}$ _____

Improper Fractions and Mixed Numbers

An **improper fraction** has a numerator that is greater than or equal to its denominator. It has a value greater than or equal to one. A **mixed number** combines a whole number and a fraction.

━━ Example ━━━━━━

Write an improper fraction and a mixed number to describe the picture.

The shapes are divided into fifths, so the denominator of all fractions will be 5.

There are 12 shaded parts, so the numerator will be 12.

The improper fraction shown by the picture is $\frac{12}{5}$.

There are 2 wholes shaded. The third shape has 2 fifths shaded.

The mixed number shown by the picture is $2\frac{2}{5}$.

Try It Write an improper fraction and a mixed number to describe each picture.

a.

_____

b.

_____

c.

_____

d.

_____

e.

_____

f.

_____

g.

_____

h.

_____

Name _____

Converting Fractions and Decimals

Fractions and decimals can be used to name the same number.
Sometimes it is necessary to write a fraction as a decimal or a
decimal as a fraction.

━ Example 1 ━

To write a fraction as a decimal, divide the numerator by
the denominator. Your answer will be a **terminating decimal,**
one with no remainder, or a **repeating decimal,** one that repeats
a pattern.

a. Write $\frac{2}{5}$ as a decimal.

Divide 2 by 5.

$$\begin{array}{r} 0.4 \\ 5\overline{)2.0} \\ \underline{2\,0} \end{array}$$

The fraction $\frac{2}{5}$ and the decimal 0.4
name the same number.

b. Write $\frac{2}{9}$ as a decimal.

Divide 2 by 9.

$$\begin{array}{r} 0.222... \\ 9\overline{)2.000} \\ \underline{1\,8} \\ 20 \\ \underline{18} \\ 20 \end{array}$$

The fraction $\frac{2}{9}$ and the decimal 0.222...
name the same number.

Try It Write as a decimal.

a. $\frac{4}{5}$ _____ **b.** $\frac{2}{3}$ _____ **c.** $\frac{4}{9}$ _____ **d.** $\frac{3}{8}$ _____

e. $\frac{5}{25}$ _____ **f.** $\frac{5}{6}$ _____ **g.** $\frac{5}{75}$ _____ **h.** $\frac{2}{11}$ _____

━ Example 2 ━

To write a terminating decimal as a fraction, write the digits in the
decimal as the numerator. Use the place value of the decimal to
write the denominator. Then write your answer in lowest terms.

Write 0.3 as a fraction.

$$0.3 = \frac{3}{10} \longleftarrow \text{place value of decimal}$$

The fraction is in lowest terms, so the decimal 0.3 and the
fraction $\frac{3}{10}$ name the same number.

Try It Write as a fraction in lowest terms.

i. 0.45 _____ **j.** 0.25 _____ **k.** 0.6 _____ **l.** 0.52 _____

m. 0.01 _____ **n.** 0.24 _____ **o.** 0.625 _____ **p.** 0.440 _____

Comparing and Ordering

Sometimes it is necessary to compare or order fractions. One way to do this is to write each fraction so that they have the same, or a **common, denominator.** For example, the fractions $\frac{4}{10}$ and $\frac{8}{10}$ have a common denominator, tenths.

━━ Example 1 ━━

Find a common denominator for $\frac{3}{4}$ and $\frac{2}{3}$.

One way to find a common denominator of $\frac{3}{4}$ and $\frac{2}{3}$ is to list the multiples of both denominators.

Multiples of 4: 4, 8, **12**, 16
Multiples of 3: 3, 6, 9, **12**

A common multiple is 12, so a common denominator is also 12.

Try It Find a common denominator.

a. $\frac{1}{2}, \frac{3}{5}$ _____

b. $\frac{3}{4}, \frac{1}{7}$ _____

c. $\frac{4}{10}, \frac{3}{8}$ _____

d. $\frac{7}{10}, \frac{2}{3}$ _____

e. $\frac{3}{4}, \frac{3}{10}$ _____

f. $\frac{11}{20}, \frac{9}{15}$ _____

g. $\frac{3}{8}, \frac{1}{9}$ _____

h. $\frac{4}{5}, \frac{3}{4}$ _____

i. $\frac{5}{12}, \frac{7}{8}$ _____

━━ Example 2 ━━

Compare $\frac{3}{4}$ and $\frac{5}{6}$.

$$\frac{3}{4} \quad \boxed{?} \quad \frac{5}{6}$$

Write the fractions using a common denominator ⟶ $\frac{9}{12} < \frac{10}{12}$ ⟵ Since the denominators are the same, compare the numerators.

$9 < 10$ so $\frac{9}{12} < \frac{10}{12}$ and $\frac{3}{4} < \frac{5}{6}$.

Try It Compare the fractions. Use $>$, $<$, or $=$.

j. $\frac{3}{12}$ ___ $\frac{5}{12}$

k. $\frac{1}{6}$ ___ $\frac{1}{4}$

l. $\frac{2}{3}$ ___ $\frac{1}{2}$

m. $\frac{3}{8}$ ___ $\frac{3}{4}$

n. $\frac{9}{10}$ ___ $\frac{4}{5}$

o. $\frac{5}{12}$ ___ $\frac{3}{8}$

p. $\frac{3}{6}$ ___ $\frac{1}{2}$

q. $\frac{5}{8}$ ___ $\frac{1}{3}$

r. $\frac{2}{5}$ ___ $\frac{1}{2}$

s. $\frac{2}{3}$ ___ $\frac{5}{8}$

t. $\frac{4}{7}$ ___ $\frac{2}{3}$

u. $\frac{3}{4}$ ___ $\frac{5}{6}$

Name _____

Adding and Subtracting Fractions with Like Denominators

Two fractions with the same denominator have **like denominators**.

When adding and subtracting fractions with like denominators, the denominator acts like a label, telling you what size pieces you are using. The numerators are the number of pieces you add or subtract.

━━ Example 1 ━━

Simplify $\frac{5}{8} + \frac{1}{8}$.

Add numerators only.

Denominators do not change.

Write in lowest terms.

$$\frac{5}{8} + \frac{1}{8} = \frac{5+1}{8}$$
$$= \frac{6}{8}$$
$$= \frac{3}{4}$$

So, $\frac{5}{8} + \frac{1}{8} = \frac{3}{4}$.

Try It Simplify. Draw a picture if you like. Write each answer in lowest terms.

a. $\frac{3}{8} + \frac{2}{8}$ _____

b. $\frac{1}{3} + \frac{1}{3}$ _____

c. $\frac{13}{20} + \frac{5}{20}$ _____

d. $\frac{5}{12} + \frac{1}{12}$ _____

e. $\frac{1}{5} + \frac{2}{5}$ _____

f. $\frac{1}{6} + \frac{1}{6}$ _____

g. $\frac{5}{9} + \frac{1}{9}$ _____

h. $\frac{7}{15} + \frac{2}{15}$ _____

━━ Example 2 ━━

Simplify $\frac{9}{10} - \frac{3}{10}$.

Subtract numerators only.

Denominators do not change.

Write in lowest terms.

$$\frac{9}{10} - \frac{3}{10} = \frac{9-3}{10}$$
$$= \frac{6}{10}$$
$$= \frac{3}{5}$$

So, $\frac{9}{10} - \frac{3}{10} = \frac{3}{5}$.

Try It Simplify. Draw a picture if you like. Write each answer in lowest terms.

i. $\frac{9}{15} - \frac{5}{15}$ _____

j. $\frac{7}{8} - \frac{1}{8}$ _____

k. $\frac{4}{5} - \frac{3}{5}$ _____

l. $\frac{9}{7} - \frac{5}{7}$ _____

m. $\frac{3}{4} - \frac{1}{4}$ _____

n. $\frac{7}{10} - \frac{3}{10}$ _____

o. $\frac{6}{7} - \frac{3}{7}$ _____

p. $\frac{11}{12} - \frac{5}{12}$ _____

Adding and Subtracting Fractions with Unlike Denominators

Fractions with different denominators, or **unlike denominators,** represent pieces of different sizes. In order to add or subtract fractions with unlike denominators, you need to change them to equivalent fractions with the same denominator.

You can find equivalent fractions by either multiplying or dividing the numerator and the denominator of a fraction by the same nonzero number. The **least common denominator** of two fractions is the least common multiple of the two denominators.

▬ Example ▬

Simplify $\frac{3}{4} - \frac{1}{2}$.

Find the least common denominator for $\frac{3}{4}$ and $\frac{1}{2}$ by listing multiples of both denominators.

Multiples of 4:   **4**,   8,   12,   16
Multiples of 2:   2,   **4**,   6,   8

The least common multiple of 4 and 2 is 4. So, 4 is also the least common denominator. Only $\frac{1}{2}$ needs to be changed to an equivalent fraction.

Multiply numerator and denominator by 2 to make the denominator 4.

$$\frac{1}{2} = \frac{1 \times 2}{2 \times 2} = \frac{2}{4}$$

Rewrite the expression using equivalent fractions. $\frac{3}{4} - \frac{1}{2} = \frac{3}{4} - \frac{2}{4}$

Subtract. $\frac{3-2}{4} = \frac{1}{4}$

Since $\frac{1}{4}$ is in lowest terms, $\frac{3}{4} - \frac{1}{2} = \frac{1}{4}$.

Try It Simplify $\frac{5}{12} + \frac{1}{4}$.

   a. Find the least common multiple of 12 and 4. _____

   b. Write as equivalent fractions. $\frac{5}{12} = $ _____ $\frac{1}{4} = $ _____

   c. Rewrite the expression. _____

   d. Add. Write in lowest terms. _____

Simplify.

   e. $\frac{5}{6} - \frac{2}{3}$ _____   **f.** $\frac{3}{8} + \frac{1}{4}$ _____   **g.** $\frac{2}{3} - \frac{1}{5}$ _____

   h. $\frac{1}{12} + \frac{2}{3}$ _____   **i.** $\frac{3}{5} - \frac{1}{10}$ _____   **j.** $\frac{7}{10} - \frac{1}{4}$ _____

Solving Fraction Equations: Addition and Subtraction

You can use mental math to solve addition and subtraction equations involving fractions with like denominators. To solve equations involving fractions with unlike denominators, you need to change the fractions to equivalent fractions with like denominators.

━ Example ━

Solve $x - \frac{3}{8} = \frac{5}{16}$.

Use 16 as the LCD (least common denominator). Change $\frac{3}{8}$ to an equivalent fraction.

$$\frac{3}{8} = \frac{3 \times 2}{8 \times 2} = \frac{6}{16}$$

Read as "What number minus $\frac{6}{16}$ equals $\frac{5}{16}$?"

$$x - \frac{6}{16} = \frac{5}{16}$$

Use mental math.

$$\frac{11}{16} - \frac{6}{16} = \frac{5}{16}$$

Check to see that the equation is true.

$$\frac{5}{16} = \frac{5}{16}\checkmark$$

So, $x = \frac{11}{16}$.

Try It Solve each equation. Write each answer in the lowest terms.

a. $a + \frac{1}{5} = \frac{4}{5}$

What number plus $\frac{1}{5}$ equals $\frac{4}{5}$? _____ So, $a =$ _____.

Show that the equation is true. _____

b. $k - \frac{1}{3} = \frac{2}{9}$

What is the least common multiple of 3 and 9? _____

Rewrite the equation using like denominators. _____

What number minus $\frac{3}{9}$ equals $\frac{2}{9}$? _____ So, $k =$ _____

Show that the equation is true. _____

c. $\frac{1}{4} + x = \frac{3}{4}$ $x =$ _____

d. $y - \frac{5}{8} = \frac{1}{8}$ $y =$ _____

e. $\frac{7}{10} - c = \frac{2}{5}$ $c =$ _____

f. $\frac{5}{12} + r = \frac{7}{3}$ $r =$ _____

g. $\frac{1}{12} + b = \frac{1}{4}$ $b =$ _____

h. $s - \frac{1}{2} = \frac{1}{6}$ $s =$ _____

i. $d + \frac{1}{3} = \frac{7}{12}$ $d =$ _____

j. $\frac{5}{6} - f = \frac{7}{12}$ $f =$ _____

k. $s + \frac{3}{8} = \frac{3}{4}$ $s =$ _____

l. $t - \frac{3}{10} = \frac{5}{8}$ $t =$ _____

Estimation: Sums and Differences of Mixed Numbers

A *mixed number* is a number like $6\frac{3}{8}$ that contains a whole number and a fraction. You can estimate sums and differences of mixed numbers by rounding each mixed number to the nearest whole number.

To round a mixed number, look at the fractional part of the mixed number. Drop the fraction and leave the whole number unchanged if the fractional part is less than $\frac{1}{2}$. Round up to the next whole number if the fractional part is $\frac{1}{2}$ or greater.

Example 1

Round $4\frac{1}{3}$ to the nearest whole number.

The numerator of the fraction, 1, is less than half the denominator. So, $\frac{1}{3}$ is less than $\frac{1}{2}$. Drop the fraction.

Round $4\frac{1}{3}$ down to 4.

Try It Round to the nearest whole number.

a. $1\frac{3}{4}$ 3 is more than half of 4, so $1\frac{3}{4}$ rounds to _____.

b. $8\frac{1}{8}$ _____   c. $2\frac{1}{3}$ _____   d. $14\frac{4}{6}$ _____   e. $9\frac{4}{8}$ _____

Example 2

Estimate $1\frac{1}{4} + 3\frac{7}{8}$.

Round each number to the nearest whole number by comparing the numerator to the denominator.

Since 1 is less than half of 4, drop the fraction. $1\frac{1}{4} \rightarrow 1$

Since 7 is more than half of 8, round to the next whole number. $3\frac{7}{8} \rightarrow 4$

Estimate by adding the two whole numbers: $1 + 4 = 5$.

An estimate of the sum of $1\frac{1}{4} + 3\frac{7}{8}$ is 5.

Try It Estimate.

f. $4\frac{5}{8} - 2\frac{1}{3}$ Round $4\frac{5}{8}$. _____   Round $2\frac{1}{3}$. _____   Estimate. _____

g. $9\frac{4}{5} - 3\frac{1}{2}$ _____   h. $11\frac{3}{4} + 4\frac{2}{11}$ _____

i. $7\frac{5}{9} - 4\frac{7}{10}$ _____   j. $6\frac{3}{8} + 5\frac{6}{12}$ _____

k. $8\frac{3}{8} - 7\frac{1}{5}$ _____   l. $17\frac{5}{6} - 10\frac{1}{8}$ _____

Adding Mixed Numbers

Just as you can add whole numbers and add fractions, you can add
mixed numbers. To add mixed numbers:

1. Add the whole numbers.
2. Add the fractions.
3. Put the two parts together.

If the sum of the fractions is an improper fraction, you may need to
rewrite it as a mixed number and add the whole number parts together.

▬ Example ▬

Add $1\frac{1}{2} + 3\frac{5}{6}$. Write the sum as a whole or mixed number in lowest terms.

Rewrite the fractions using their LCD 6.

$$1\frac{1}{2} \rightarrow 1\frac{3}{6}$$
$$+ 3\frac{5}{6} \rightarrow + 3\frac{5}{6}$$

Add the whole numbers. Then add the fractions.

Rewrite the improper fraction as a mixed number.

Add the whole number parts. Write the sum in lowest terms.

$$4\frac{8}{6}$$
$$4 + 1\frac{2}{6}$$
$$5\frac{2}{6} = 5\frac{1}{3}$$

So, $1\frac{1}{2} + 3\frac{5}{6} = 5\frac{1}{3}$.

Try It Add. Write each sum as a whole or mixed number in lowest terms.

a. $8\frac{1}{5} + 12\frac{3}{5}$ The fractions have like denominators.

Add the whole numbers. _____ Add the fractions. _____

Add the two parts. _____

b. $12\frac{3}{4} + 3\frac{1}{2}$ Rewrite using the LCD. _____

Add the whole numbers. _____ Add the fractions. _____

Rewrite as mixed number. _____

Add the whole number parts. Write the sum in lowest terms. _____

c. $4\frac{7}{8} + 2\frac{3}{4}$ _____

d. $5\frac{2}{3} + 7\frac{1}{12}$ _____

e. $1\frac{1}{2} + 1\frac{1}{2}$ _____

f. $2\frac{2}{5} + 3\frac{2}{5}$ _____

g. $4\frac{1}{6} + 2\frac{2}{3}$ _____

h. $3\frac{5}{8} + 5\frac{3}{4}$ _____

i. $6\frac{1}{4} + 7\frac{5}{6}$ _____

j. $9\frac{2}{9} + 7\frac{2}{3}$ _____

Subtracting Mixed Numbers

Just as you can subtract whole numbers and fractions, you can subtract mixed numbers. If the fraction to be subtracted is larger than the other fraction, you must rename part of the whole number as a fraction. Remember that 1 equals a fraction with the same number as the numerator and denominator.

▬ Example 1 ▬

Rename $4\frac{2}{3}$ as $3\frac{\square}{\square}$.

Rename 4 as $3 + \frac{3}{3}$ and add to $\frac{2}{3}$: $3 + \frac{3}{3} + \frac{2}{3} = 3\frac{5}{3}$.

So, $4\frac{2}{3} = 3\frac{5}{3}$.

Try It Rename each number.

a. $2\frac{4}{5} = 1\frac{\square}{5}$ _____

b. $10\frac{1}{2} = 9\frac{\square}{2}$ _____

c. $16\frac{5}{8} = 15\frac{\square}{8}$ _____

▬ Example 2 ▬

Subtract $8\frac{1}{3} - 2\frac{5}{6}$. Write the answer as a whole or mixed number in lowest terms.

Rewrite fractions using LCD. LCD is 6.	Rename $8\frac{2}{6}$ as $7 + \frac{6}{6} + \frac{2}{6}$, or $7\frac{8}{6}$.	Subtract the whole numbers.	Subtract the fractions.

$$8\frac{1}{3} \rightarrow 8\frac{2}{6} \rightarrow 7\frac{8}{6} \rightarrow 7\frac{8}{6} \rightarrow 7\frac{8}{6}$$
$$-2\frac{5}{6} \rightarrow -2\frac{5}{6} \rightarrow -2\frac{5}{6} \rightarrow -2\frac{5}{6} \rightarrow -2\frac{5}{6}$$
$$ 5 \qquad 5\frac{3}{6}$$

Write the difference as a mixed number in lowest terms. $5\frac{3}{6} = 5\frac{1}{2}$

So, $8\frac{1}{3} - 2\frac{5}{6} = 5\frac{1}{2}$.

Try It Subtract. Write each difference as a whole or mixed number in lowest terms.

d. $7\frac{1}{5} - 2\frac{3}{5}$

Rename $7\frac{1}{5}$. $7\frac{1}{5} = 6\frac{\square}{5}$. _____   Subtract the whole numbers. _____

Subtract the fractions. _____   Write the difference. _____

e. $14\frac{3}{5} - 7\frac{3}{10}$ _____

f. $6\frac{1}{4} - 2\frac{3}{4}$ _____

g. $9\frac{2}{3} - 5\frac{3}{4}$ _____

h. $10 - 3\frac{5}{6}$ _____

i. $5\frac{7}{8} - 2\frac{1}{4}$ _____

j. $8\frac{1}{5} - 7\frac{3}{4}$ _____

k. $10\frac{5}{9} - 6\frac{2}{3}$ _____

l. $12 - 5\frac{3}{5}$ _____

m. $15\frac{2}{3} - 15\frac{1}{6}$ _____

n. $20\frac{5}{8} - \frac{3}{4}$ _____

Estimation: Products and Quotients of Fractions

You can use rounding to estimate products and quotients of fractions and mixed numbers.

- Round each factor to the nearest whole number.

- Multiply or divide the whole numbers.

▬ Example 1 ▬

Estimate: $4\frac{3}{5} \times 2\frac{3}{8}$.

$$4\frac{3}{5} \qquad \times \qquad 2\frac{3}{8}$$

$\frac{3}{5} > \frac{1}{2}$ $\frac{3}{8} < \frac{1}{2}$

Round up.   Round down.

$$5 \qquad \times \qquad 2 \qquad = \qquad 10$$ So, the estimate of $4\frac{3}{5} \times 2\frac{3}{8}$ is 10.

Try It

Estimate: $4\frac{2}{3} \times 5\frac{4}{9}$.

a. Round to the nearest whole number: $4\frac{2}{3} \rightarrow$ _____ $5\frac{4}{9} \rightarrow$ _____

b. Multiply. _____ $\times$ _____ = _____

Estimate.

c. $3\frac{7}{9} \times 5\frac{4}{15}$ _____

d. $8\frac{4}{9} \times 6\frac{5}{8}$ _____

▬ Example 2 ▬

Estimate: $9\frac{7}{16} \div 2\frac{2}{3}$.

$$9\frac{7}{16} \qquad \div \qquad 2\frac{2}{3}$$

$\frac{7}{16} < \frac{1}{2}$ $\frac{2}{3} > \frac{1}{2}$

Round down.   Round up.

$$9 \qquad \div \qquad 3 \qquad = \qquad 3$$ So, the estimate of $9\frac{7}{16} \div 2\frac{2}{3}$ is 3.

Try It

Estimate: $12\frac{3}{14} \div 3\frac{7}{8}$.

e. Round to the nearest whole number: $12\frac{3}{14} \rightarrow$ _____ $3\frac{7}{8} \rightarrow$ _____

f. Divide. _____ $\div$ _____ = _____

Estimate.

g. $14\frac{7}{8} \div 5\frac{2}{5}$ _____

h. $75\frac{5}{24} \div 24\frac{17}{30}$ _____

Multiplying by a Whole Number

To multiply a fraction or mixed number by a whole number, first write both numbers as fractions. Then write the product of the numerators over the product of the denominators. Simplify if necessary.

━━ Example 1 ━━

Multiply: $6 \times \frac{3}{4}$.

Write the whole number as an improper fraction.

Multiply the numerators. Then multiply the denominators.

Multiply and simplify.

So, $6 \times \frac{3}{4} = 4\frac{1}{2}$.

$$6 \times \frac{3}{4} = \frac{6}{1} \times \frac{3}{4}$$
$$= \frac{6 \times 3}{1 \times 4}$$
$$= \frac{18}{4} = 4\frac{2}{4} = 4\frac{1}{2}$$

━━ Example 2 ━━

Multiply: $4 \times 1\frac{3}{5}$.

Write the mixed number as an improper fraction.

Multiply the numerators. Then multiply the denominators.

Simplify.

So, $4 \times 1\frac{3}{5} = 6\frac{2}{5}$.

$$4 \times 1\frac{3}{5} = \frac{4}{1} \times \frac{8}{5}$$
$$= \frac{4 \times 8}{1 \times 5}$$
$$= \frac{32}{5} = 6\frac{2}{5}$$

Try It

Multiply: $\frac{2}{3} \times 5$.

a. Write the whole number as an improper fraction. $5 = $ _____

b. Multiply numerators and denominators. _____ $\times$ _____ = _____

c. Simplify. _____

Multiply.

d. $\frac{3}{8} \times 9$ _____

e. $8 \times \frac{3}{5}$ _____

f. $1\frac{1}{2} \times 8$ _____

g. $\frac{5}{8} \times 9$ _____

h. $12 \times \frac{4}{5}$ _____

i. $1\frac{1}{2} \times 7$ _____

j. $2 \times \frac{5}{6}$ _____

k. $9 \times 3\frac{2}{3}$ _____

Multiplying by a Fraction

You can multiply two fractions by writing the product of the numerators over the product of the denominators.

▬ Example ▬

Multiply: $1\frac{1}{2} \times 3\frac{1}{2}$.

Write each mixed number as an improper fraction.

$$1\frac{1}{2} \times 3\frac{1}{2} =$$
$$\downarrow \qquad \downarrow$$

Multiply the numerators. Then multiply the denominators.

$$\frac{3}{2} \times \frac{7}{2} = \frac{3}{2} \times \frac{7}{2}$$

Multiply and simplify.

$$= \frac{21}{4} = 5\frac{1}{4}$$

So, $1\frac{1}{2} \times 3\frac{1}{2} = 5\frac{1}{4}$.

Try It

Multiply: $\frac{3}{5} \times \frac{7}{12}$.

a. Multiply numerators and denominators. _____ × _____ = _____

b. Simplify. _____

Multiply: $\frac{7}{8} \times 1\frac{1}{4}$.

c. Write the mixed number as an improper fraction. $1\frac{1}{4} =$ _____

d. Multiply numerators and denominators. _____ × _____ = _____

e. Simplify. _____

Multiply: $1\frac{3}{4} \times 2\frac{1}{2}$.

f. Write the whole numbers as improper fractions. $1\frac{3}{4} =$ _____ $2\frac{1}{2} =$ _____

g. Multiply numerators and denominators. _____ × _____ = _____

h. Simplify. _____

Multiply.

i. $\frac{1}{4} \times \frac{9}{10}$ _____

j. $\frac{5}{6} \times \frac{2}{3}$ _____

k. $\frac{3}{5} \times 1\frac{3}{5}$ _____

l. $2\frac{1}{2} \times \frac{7}{8}$ _____

m. $2\frac{3}{5} \times 1\frac{1}{3}$ _____

n. $\frac{9}{10} \times \frac{4}{5}$ _____

o. Amal's bones make up about $\frac{1}{5}$ of his body weight. He weighs $158\frac{1}{2}$ pounds. How much do his bones weigh? _____

Dividing Whole Numbers by Fractions

Dividing by a fraction is the same as multiplying by its **reciprocal.**
Reciprocals are numbers whose numerators and denominators have
been switched. When two numbers are reciprocals, their product is 1.
For example, $\frac{2}{3}$ and $\frac{3}{2}$ are reciprocals because $\frac{2}{3} \times \frac{3}{2}$ is 1.

Study these whole numbers to learn how to divide by fractions.

$$8 \div \boxed{4} = 2$$
$$8 \times \boxed{\frac{1}{4}} = 2$$

4 and $\frac{1}{4}$ are reciprocals.

$$7 \div \boxed{8} = \frac{7}{8}$$
$$7 \times \boxed{\frac{1}{8}} = \frac{7}{8}$$

8 and $\frac{1}{8}$ are reciprocals.

▬ Example ▬

Divide: $4 \div \frac{3}{8}$.

Write 4 as an improper fraction.
Multiply by the reciprocal of $\frac{3}{8}$.
The reciprocal of $\frac{3}{8}$ is $\frac{8}{3}$.

Simplify.

So, $4 \div \frac{3}{8} = 10\frac{2}{3}$.

$$4 \boxed{\div \frac{3}{8}} = \frac{4}{1} \boxed{\times \frac{8}{3}}$$
$$= \frac{32}{3} = 10\frac{2}{3}$$

Try It

a. Divide: $21 \div \frac{4}{3}$.

Improper   Reciprocal
fraction

Multiply. _____ × _____ = _____ = _____

b. Divide: $10 \div \frac{4}{3}$.

Improper   Reciprocal
fraction

Multiply. _____ × _____ = _____ = _____ = _____

Divide.

c. $3 \div \frac{3}{7}$ _____

d. $6 \div \frac{2}{5}$ _____

e. $8 \div \frac{6}{7}$ _____

f. $20 \div \frac{3}{5}$ _____

g. $4 \div \frac{5}{6}$ _____

h. $25 \div \frac{5}{8}$ _____

i. $12 \div \frac{2}{3}$ _____

j. $16 \div \frac{4}{9}$ _____

Dividing Fractions by Fractions

Dividing by a fraction is the same as multiplying by its reciprocal.
For example, $\frac{3}{5} \div \frac{2}{3}$ is the same as $\frac{3}{5} \times \frac{3}{2}$.

▬ Example ▬

Divide: $2\frac{4}{5} \div \frac{3}{4}$.

Write $2\frac{4}{5}$ as an improper fraction.
Multiply by the reciprocal of $\frac{3}{4}$.

Simplify.

So, $2\frac{4}{5} \div \frac{3}{4} = 3\frac{11}{15}$.

$$2\frac{4}{5} \boxed{\div \frac{3}{4}} = \frac{14}{5} \boxed{\times \frac{4}{3}}$$

$$= \frac{56}{15}$$

$$= 3\frac{11}{15}$$

Try It

a. Divide: $\frac{1}{2} \div \frac{4}{5}$.

Reciprocal

Multiply by the reciprocal of $\frac{4}{5}$. _____ × _____ = _____

b. Divide: $\frac{3}{8} \div 3$.

Write the divisor as an improper fraction. _____

Reciprocal

Multiply by the reciprocal of the divisor. _____ × _____ = _____

= _____

c. Divide: $3\frac{9}{10} \div \frac{2}{3}$.

Write the mixed number as an improper fraction. _____

Write the reciprocal of the divisor. _____

Multiply. _____ × _____ = _____

Divide. Remember to simplify if necessary.

d. $\frac{7}{8} \div \frac{2}{3}$ _____

e. $\frac{2}{5} \div \frac{3}{4}$ _____

f. $\frac{4}{7} \div 2$ _____

g. $3\frac{1}{3} \div \frac{4}{5}$ _____

h. $2\frac{3}{8} \div \frac{1}{10}$ _____

i. $15 \div 2\frac{1}{2}$ _____

j. $4\frac{1}{5} \div \frac{7}{8}$ _____

k. $1\frac{3}{4} \div 1\frac{2}{5}$ _____

Solving Fraction Equations: Multiplication and Division

When solving multiplication equations, it may help to first find the numerator of the missing value and then the denominator. If the equation includes whole numbers or mixed numbers, you may need to rewrite these numbers as fractions.

━ Example 1 ━

Solve: $\frac{2}{5}x = \frac{4}{25}$.

Think: What number times $\frac{2}{5}$ equals $\frac{4}{25}$?
Then use mental math to find the numerator.

Use mental math to find the denominator.

$(2 \times 2 = 4)$

$\frac{2}{5} \times \frac{?}{?} = \frac{4}{25}$

$\frac{2}{5} \times \frac{2}{?} = \frac{4}{25}$

$(5 \times 5 = 25)$

Check to see that the equation is true.

So, $x = \frac{2}{5}$.

$\frac{2}{5} \times \frac{2}{5} = \frac{4}{25}$ ✓

Try It Solve for x.

a. $\frac{2}{3}x = \frac{8}{15}$ $x =$ _____

b. $\frac{3}{4}x = \frac{9}{20}$ $x =$ _____

c. $\frac{1}{3}x = 4$ $x =$ _____

d. $\frac{3}{8}x = \frac{18}{16}$ $x =$ _____

━ Example 2 ━

Solve: $x \div \frac{3}{4} = \frac{8}{9}$.

Rewrite as a multiplication equation.

Use mental math to find the numerator.

Use mental math to find the denominator.

Check to see that the equation is true.

So, $x = \frac{2}{3}$.

$(2 \times 4 = 8)$

$\frac{?}{?} \times \frac{4}{3} = \frac{8}{9}$

$(3 \times 3 = 9)$

$\frac{2}{3} \div \frac{3}{4} = \frac{8}{9}$ ✓

Try It Solve for x.

e. $x \div \frac{2}{3} = \frac{6}{10}$ $x =$ _____

f. $x \div \frac{5}{9} = \frac{9}{25}$ $x =$ _____

g. $x \div \frac{3}{8} = \frac{16}{27}$ $x =$ _____

h. $x \div \frac{4}{5} = \frac{35}{48}$ $x =$ _____

i. $x \div \frac{7}{9} = \frac{27}{35}$ $x =$ _____

j. $x \div \frac{3}{10} = \frac{20}{27}$ $x =$ _____

Classifying Lines

A **line** extends forever in both directions.

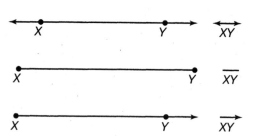

A line **segment** has two **endpoints**. The segment does not extend beyond these endpoints.

A **ray** has one endpoint, and extends forever in the other direction.

If lines cross through the same point, they **intersect.** If they intersect at right angles, they are **perpendicular**. If they do not intersect no matter how far they extend, they are **parallel.**

The lines intersect.   The lines are perpendicular.   The lines are parallel.

Rays and segments can also intersect, be perpendicular or parallel.

━ Example 1 ━

State whether the figure is a line, a ray, or a segment.

The figure has one endpoint, and extends forever in the other direction, so the figure is a ray.

Try It State whether each figure is a line, a ray, or a segment.

a.   b.    c.    d.

_____   _____   _____   _____

━ Example 2 ━

Describe the relationship between the line segments.

The segments intersect at right angles, so the segments are perpendicular.

Try It Describe the relationship between the lines, rays, or segments.

e.   f.   g.    h.

_____   _____   _____   _____

Name _____

Classifying Angles

An **angle** is formed by two rays with the same
endpoint. The rays are the **sides** of the angle.
The common endpoint is the **vertex**.

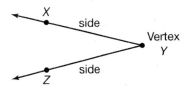

You can name an angle using a point on each side and the vertex. The
vertex must appear as the middle letter. When it is not confusing, you
can name an angle using the vertex alone. The angle shown can be
called ∠XYZ, ∠ZYX, or ∠Y.

Angles can be classified by their size.

 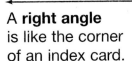 

An **acute angle**
is smaller than a
right angle.

A **right angle**
is like the corner
of an index card.

An **obtuse angle**
is greater than a
right angle but
smaller than a
straight angle.

A **straight angle**
is a line.

▬ Example 1 ▬

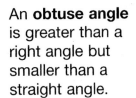

Name the angle in three ways.

The vertex is S.

The angle can be named ∠UST, ∠TSU, or ∠S.

Try It Name each angle in three ways.

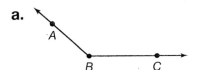

a.

b.

c.

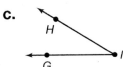

▬ Example 2 ▬

Classify ∠W as acute, right, obtuse or straight.

Since the angle is smaller than a right angle, it is acute.

Try It Classify each angle as acute, right, obtuse, or straight.

d.

e.

f.

g.

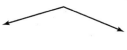

Measuring Angles

Angles are measured in units called **degrees.** Use the symbol ° to indicate degrees. A complete circle measures 360°.

An **acute angle** measures more than 0° and less than 90.

A **right angle** measures exactly 90°.

An **obtuse angle** measures more than 90° and less than 180°.

A **protractor** is a tool that measures angles.

━━ Example ━━

What is the measure of ∠FGH?

Step 1: Place your protractor so that the middle mark (hole) on its bottom side is exactly on the vertex of the angle.

Step 2: Place the protractor line, with the zero mark on the scale, over one side of the angle.

Step 3: Read the number where the other side of the angle meets the degree scale on the protractor. Since the angle is an acute angle, use the smaller number in the pair.

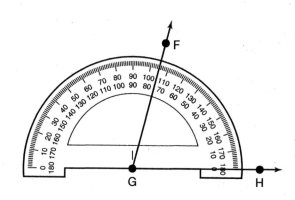

The measure of ∠FGH is 75°.

Try It Find the measure of each angle.

a.

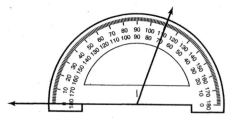

_____

b.

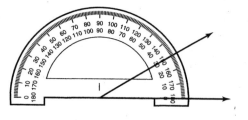

_____

c.

_____

d.

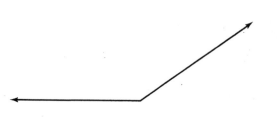

_____

Exploring Angles In a Triangle

A **triangle** is a closed figure made from three line segments. The sum of the angles in any triangle always equals 180°.

Triangles can be classified by the size of their angles.

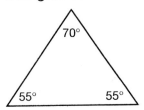

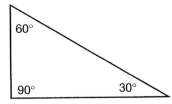

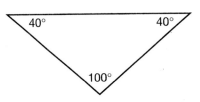

An **acute triangle** has three acute angles.

A **right triangle** has exactly one right angle.

An **obtuse triangle** has exactly one obtuse angle.

━ Example 1 ━

Classify this triangle as acute, right or obtuse.

All three angles of the triangle are less than 90°, so the triangle is acute.

Try It   Classify each triangle as acute, right, or obtuse.

a. 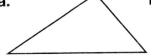   **b.**    **c.** 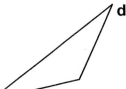   **d.**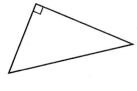

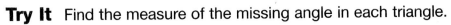

━ Example 2 ━

Find the measure of the missing angle in the triangle.

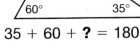

The sum of the angles of a triangle is equal to 180°.

Write an equation using the given measures.   35 + 60 + **?** = 180

Add the given measures.   95 + **?** = 180

Use mental math to find the missing measure.   95 + **85** = 180

So, the angle measures 85°.

Try It   Find the measure of the missing angle in each triangle.

e. 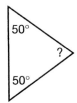   **f.** **g.** 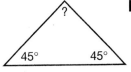   **h.**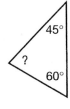

Name _____

Exploring Sides of a Triangle

Triangles can be classified by the lengths of their sides.

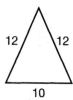

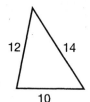

An **equilateral triangle**
has three sides of the
same length.

An **isosceles triangle**
has two sides of the
same length.

A **scalene triangle**
has no sides of
equal length.

In order for three lengths to form a triangle, the sum of the two
shortest lengths must be greater than the longest length.

━━ Example 1 ━━

Classify the triangle as scalene, equilateral, or isosceles.

None of the sides of the triangle are the same length,
so the figure is a scalene triangle.

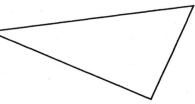

Try It Classify each triangle as scalene, equilateral, or isosceles.

a.    b.   c. 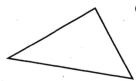   d.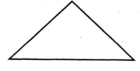

_____   _____   _____   _____

━━ Example 2 ━━

State whether these lengths can form a triangle: 19 cm, 14 cm, 28 cm.

Add the lengths of the two shortest sides.   19 + 14 = 33

Compare the sum to the lengths of the longest side.   33 > 28

Since the sum of the lengths of the two shorter sides is greater than
the length of the longest side, a triangle can be formed.

Try It State whether the given lengths can form a triangle. Write *yes* or *no.*

e. 3 in., 3 in., 3 in. Write the sum of the lengths of the two shorter sides. _____

   Compare sum to longer line's length. Can a triangle be formed? _____

f. 23 cm, 27 cm, 78 cm _____   **g.** 1.5 yd, 4.2 yd, 2.7 yd _____

h. 13 ft, 18 ft, 13 ft _____   **i.** 113 mm, 143 mm, 192 mm _____

Polygons

A **polygon** is a closed figure made of line segments. Polygons are classified by the number of sides they have. A triangle is a polygon with 3 sides. In a **regular polygon**, all the sides and all the angles have the same measures.

Irregular Polygon   Regular Polygon

A **quadrilateral** has 4 sides.

A **pentagon** has 5 sides.

A **hexagon** has 6 sides.

An **octagon** has 8 sides.

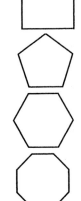

━━ Example ━━

Name the polygon and tell if it is regular or irregular.

The polygon has five sides, so it is a pentagon.
Its sides and angles are equal, so it is regular.

The polygon is a regular pentagon.

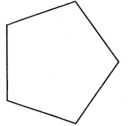

Try It   Name each polygon and tell if it is regular or irregular.

a.

b.

c.

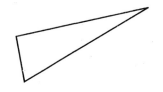

d.

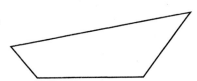

e.

f.

Name _____

Alternative Lesson 8-7

Quadrilaterals

Any **polygon** with four sides is a quadrilateral. The five special types of quadrilaterals are shown below.

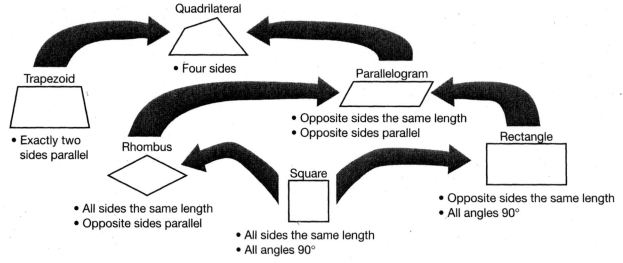

Quadrilateral
• Four sides

Trapezoid
• Exactly two sides parallel

Parallelogram
• Opposite sides the same length
• Opposite sides parallel

Rectangle
• Opposite sides the same length
• All angles 90°

Rhombus
• All sides the same length
• Opposite sides parallel

Square
• All sides the same length
• All angles 90°

Some figures can be classified in more than one way.

■ Example ■

Classify the figure in as many ways as possible.

The figure has 4 sides, so it is a quadrilateral.

The figure has opposite sides that are parallel and the same length, so it is also a parallelogram.

All angles measure 90°, and opposite sides are the same length, so it is a rectangle.

The figure is a quadrilateral, a parallelogram, and a rectangle.

Try It Classify this figure in as many ways as possible.

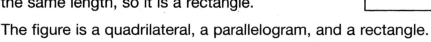

a. How many sides? _____

b. How many pairs of opposite sides are parallel? _____

c. Are opposite sides the same length? _____   **d.** Are all sides? _____

e. Do all angles measure 90°? _____

f. The polygon is a _____.

Classify this figure in as many ways as possible.

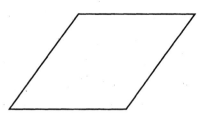

g. _____

Name _____

Flips and Line Symmetry

Two figures are **congruent** if they have the same size and shape.
A figure that can be folded into congruent halves has **line symmetry**.
A **reflection** is the mirror image of a figure that has been "flipped"
over a line.

━━ Example 1 ━━

Draw the reflection of the figure over the line.

Draw the mirror image of the figure.

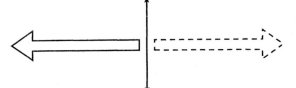

Try It Draw the reflection of each figure over the line.

a.

b.

c.

━━ Example 2 ━━

Tell if the line is a line of symmetry.

If the figure was folded at the line, the two parts
would match exactly. So, the line is a line of symmetry.

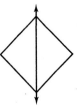

Try It Tell if each line is a line of symmetry. Write *yes* or *no*.

d.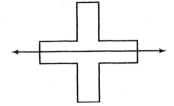

e.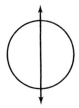

f.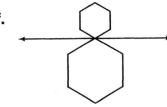

_____   _____   _____

━━ Example 3 ━━

Tell if the pair of figures is congruent.

The figures are the same shape, but are
different sizes. So, the figures are not congruent.

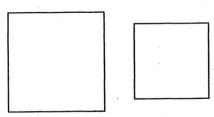

Try It Tell whether each pair of figures is congruent. Write *yes* or *no*.

g.

h.

i.

_____   _____   _____

Turns and Rotational Symmetry

A **rotation** is the image of a figure that has been turned, as if it were on a wheel. When the top of a figure turns to the right, it is turned **clockwise.** When the top turns to the left, it is turned **counter-clockwise.** You can use degrees to describe the rotation. If a figure can be rotated less than a full circle, and the rotation exactly matches the original image, then the figure has **rotational symmetry.**

━━ Example 1 ━━

Draw a 45° clockwise rotation for the figure.

The rotation is to the right. There are 360° in a circle. Draw a 45° angle to see the rotation of the figure. Then use the angle to draw the rotation.

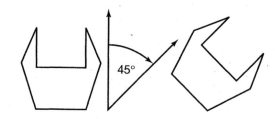

Try It Draw a 90° clockwise rotation for each figure.

a. Draw a 90° angle to see the rotation of each figure.

b.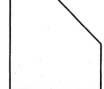

c.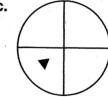

━━ Example 2 ━━

What is the least rotation that will land the figure on top of itself?

If the figure is rotated 360°, it will land on itself 2 times. The least rotation is half of 360°, or 180°.

Try It What it the least rotation that will land the figure on top of itself?

d.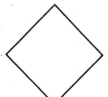

e.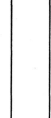

f.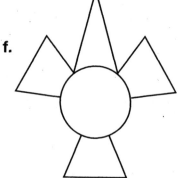

_____   _____   _____

Translations and Tessellations

When a figure is slid to a new position without flipping or turning, the new image is called a **translation.**

A pattern of congruent shapes with no gaps or overlaps, is called a **tessellation.**

━━ Example 1 ━━

State whether the one figure is a translation of the other.

The figure is in a new position.
The new position is not a flip or turn.
So, the figure is a translation.

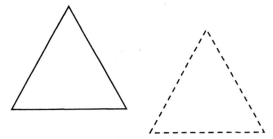

Try It State whether one figure is a translation of the other. Write *yes* or *no.*

a. Is the new position a flip? _____

Is the new position a rotation? _____

Is the new position a translation? _____

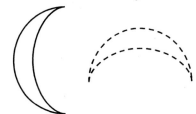

b.

c.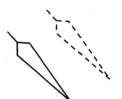

d.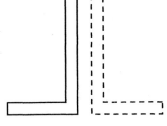

━━ Example 2 ━━

State if the figure tessellates.

The figure cannot be moved to make a pattern of congruent shapes with no gaps or overlaps, so it cannot tessellate.

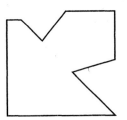

Try It Make a drawing to show whether or not each figure tessellates.

e.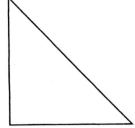

f.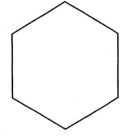

Understanding Integers

Numbers greater than 0 are known as **positive numbers**. The set
of numbers that are all *less than 0* are **negative numbers**. Negative
numbers are always shown with a minus (–) sign. Whole numbers and
their negative counterparts are known as **integers**. Zero is the only
integer that is neither positive nor negative.

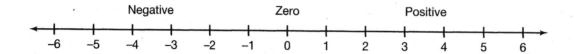

Example 1

Tell if $\frac{3}{4}$ is an integer.

Since fractions and decimals are not integers, $\frac{3}{4}$ is *not* an integer.

Try It Tell if each number is an integer. If it is not, explain why.

a. 2.4 _____

b. $3\frac{1}{3}$ _____

c. 4 _____

d. –12 _____

Example 2

Order from least to greatest: –2, 0, 5, –3, 1

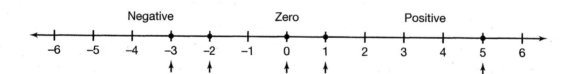

Locate the numbers on the number line. Numbers on a number line
increase from left to right. The least number is furthest to the left, so
the least number is –3. Then list the numbers as they appear from left
to right on the number line: –2, 0, 1, and 5.

The numbers in order from least to greatest are –3, –2, 0, 1, 5.

Try It Order from least to greatest. Draw a number line if you need help.

e. 8, 0, –3, –1 _____

f. –3, 5, –1, 1, –2 _____

g. 6, –2, 0, 7, –4 _____

h. 12, –15, –9, 7 _____

74

Adding Integers

The **opposite** of an integer is the integer on the opposite side of
zero but at the same distance from zero. For example, 2 and –2 are
opposites because each is the same distance from zero. The sum of
an integer and its opposite is always zero.

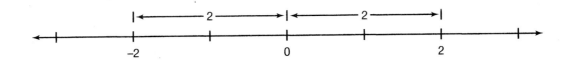

You can use different color counters or a number line to help you add.

━━ Example 1 ━━

State the opposite of 28.

The opposite of 28 is the same distance from zero as 28.
Opposite numbers have different signs.

The opposite of 28 is –28.

Try It State each number's opposite.

a. –11 _____   **b.** 32 _____   **c.** 7 _____   **d.** –9 _____

━━ Example 2 ━━

Add: 6 + (–3).

Count out or draw six same color
counters to represent +6.

Count out or draw three counters
of a different color to represent –3.

Make as many opposite pairs as
possible. Match one of each color
counter or cross out one of each
color counter in your diagram.
You can make three pairs.

Count the remaining counters.
There are 3 positive counters left,
so 6 + (–3) = 3

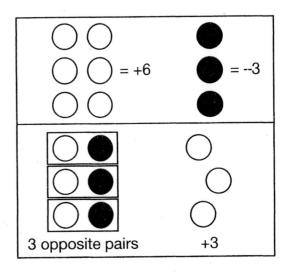

Try It Add. Use counters or draw diagrams to help.

e. –5 + (–4) _____   **f.** 5 + 3 _____   **g.** –2 + 7 _____   **h.** 8 + (–9) _____

i. –7 + 2 _____   **j.** –3 + (–7) _____   **k.** 6 + –8 _____   **l.** 4 + (–1) _____

Subtracting Integers

You can draw circles to help you subtract integers. Let a circle be +1 and a filled-in circle be –1. A circle and a filled-in circle are called a **zero pair** because their sum is zero.

To subtract integers using circles:

Step 1: Represent the first number.

Step 2: Cross out the circles representing the second number. If this is not possible, draw zero pairs until you have enough circles to cross out the second number.

Step 3: Write your answer.

━ Examples ━

Find –5 – (–3).

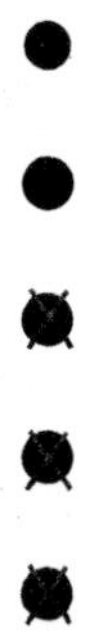

●
●
⊗
⊗
⊗

–5 – (–3) = –2.

Find –5 – 3.

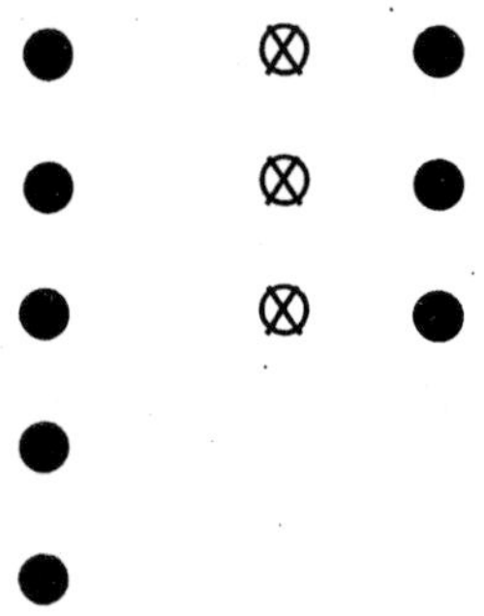

● ⊗ ●
● ⊗ ●
● ⊗ ●
●
●

–5 – 3 = –8

Find 5 – (–3).

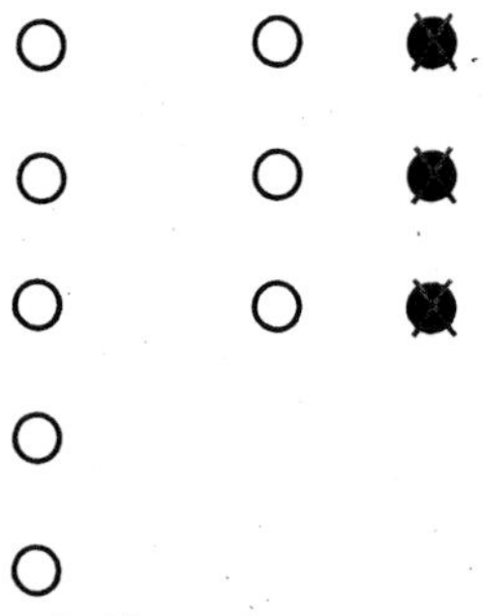

○ ○ ⊗
○ ○ ⊗
○ ○ ⊗
○
○

–5 – (–3) = 8

Try It Subtract. Use the diagram to help.

a. –2 – 5 _____

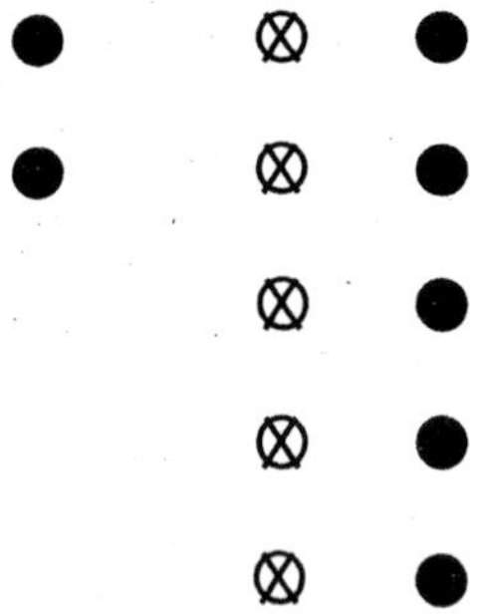

● ⊗ ●
● ⊗ ●
⊗ ●
⊗ ●
⊗ ●

b. 1 – 3 _____

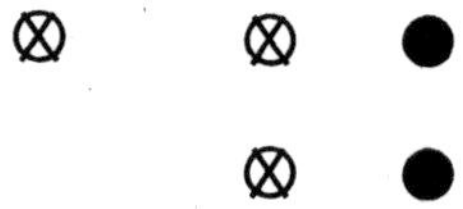

⊗ ⊗ ●
⊗ ●

Subtract. You can draw diagrams to help.

c. –4 – (–6) _____   **d.** 7 – (–2) _____   **e.** –6 – 4 _____   **f.** –2 – (–6) _____

g. 9 – (–8) _____   **h.** 4 – 1 _____   **i.** –5 – 2 _____   **j.** 4 – (–1) _____

k. –7 – (–7) _____   **l.** –3 – 1 _____   **m.** 2 – (–3) _____   **n.** +1 – 6 _____

Multiplying and Dividing Integers

Use these rules to multiply and divide integers.

When two integers have *like* signs, the product or quotient will be positive.

Both integers are positive:	$2 \times 3 = 6$	$6 \div 2 = 3$
Both integers are negative:	$-2 \times (-3) = 6$	$-6 \div (-2) = 3$

When two integers have *unlike* signs, the product or quotient will be negative.

One integer is negative, the other positive:	$-2 \times 3 = -6$	$(-6) \div 2 = -3$
One integer is positive, the other negative:	$2 \times (-3) = -6$	$6 \div (-2) = -3$

— Example 1 —

Multiply: -8×6.

Determine the numerical value of the product. $8 \times 6 = 48$

Determine the sign of the product. Since one factor is
positive and the other is negative, the product is negative. $-8 \times 6 = -48$

So, $-8 \times 6 = -48$.

Try It Multiply.

a. Will the product of $-3 \times (-5)$ be positive or negative. _____

b. Write the product of $-3 \times (-5)$. _____

c. 7×2 _____ **d.** $4 \times (-1)$ _____ **e.** $-2 \times (-2)$ _____ **f.** -2×3 _____

— Example 2 —

Divide: $-25 \div -5$.

Determine the numerical value of the quotient. $25 \div 5 = 5$

Determine the sign of the quotient. Since both
integers are negative, the quotient is positive. $-25 \div -5 = 5$

So, $-25 \div -5 = 5$.

Try It Divide.

g. Will the quotient of $72 \div (-8)$ be positive or negative. _____

h. Write the quotient of $72 \div (-8)$. _____

i. $-32 \div 8$ _____ **j.** $64 \div 8$ _____

k. $-10 \div (-10)$ _____ **l.** $-18 \div 3$ _____

Name _____

The Coordinate Plane

You can use a **coordinate plane** to locate points on the plane. The **x-axis** and the **y-axis** are number lines. They intersect at right angles at their zero points, the **origin**.

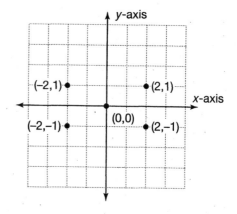

Any point can be located using an **ordered pair.** The first **coordinate** tells you how far to move on the x-axis from the origin. Coordinates of points to the right of the origin are *positive* numbers. Coordinates of points to the left are *negative* numbers. The second coordinate tells you how far to move on the y-axis from the origin. Coordinates of points up from the origin are *positive* numbers. Coordinates of points down from the origin have coordinates that are *negative* numbers.

▬ Example 1 ▬

Give the coordinates of Point A.

Start at the origin. Go right along the x-axis until you are above Point A. You move 3 units *right*, so the first coordinate is +3, or 3.

Then go down to Point A. You move 2 units *down*, so the second coordinate is –2.

The coordinates of Point A are (3, –2).

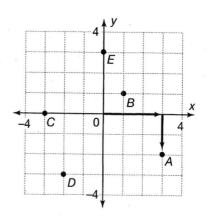

Try It Give the coordinates of each point. Use the coordinate plane above.

a. B _____   b. C _____   c. D _____   d. E _____

▬ Example 2 ▬

Plot and label Point G(–4,3)

Start at the origin. Since the first coordinate is negative, go *left* along the x-axis 4 units.

Then, since the second coordinate is positive, go *up* 3 units.

Label the point as G.

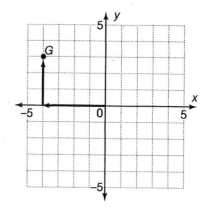

Try It Plot and label each point on the coordinate plane in Example 2.

e. H(–2, 1)   f. I(4, –2)

g. J(5, 3)   h. K(–1,–2)

78

Name _____

Graphing Slides and Flips

A *translation* slides a figure to a new position without rotating the figure. You can graph translations on a coordinate grid. Changes in the *x*-coordinate indicates movement to the right (+) or left (−). Changes in the *y*-coordinate indicates movement up (+) or down (−).

Translated figures have a specific notation. The translation of △*XYZ* is △*X'Y'Z'* , which is read as "triangle X prime Y prime Z prime."

▬ Example 1 ▬

The coordinates of *P* are (2, 1). State the coordinates of the image of Point *P* translated 2 units down.

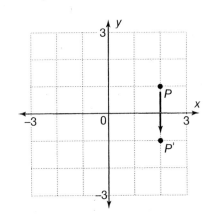

Since the slide is down, the values of the *y*-coordinate will change. To show movement *down*, *subtract* 2 from the value of the *y*-coordinate.

$P(2, 1) \rightarrow P'(2, \mathbf{1 - 2}) = P'(2, \mathbf{-1})$

So *P'* has the coordinates (2, −1).

Try It State the coordinates of the image of each point translated 1 unit left.

a. (2, 3) _____

b. (−1, 0) _____

c. (4, −3) _____

▬ Example 2 ▬

Plot the image of △*RST* by translating the figure 3 units right.

△*RST* has coordinates *R* (−2, 3), *S* (0, 4), and *T* (2, −1)

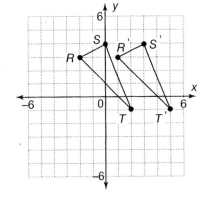

Since the triangle is to be translated to the right, the values of the *x*-coordinates will change. There is no movement up or down, so the value of the *y*-coordinates will not change.

To show the movement to the *right*, *add* 3 to the value of each *x*-coordinate.

Then plot the coordinates of △*R'S'T'*.

$R(-2, 3) \rightarrow R'(\mathbf{-2 + 3}, 3) = R'(\mathbf{1}, 3)$
$S(0, 4) \rightarrow S'(\mathbf{0 + 3}, 4) = S'(\mathbf{3}, 4)$
$T(2, -1) \rightarrow T'(\mathbf{2 + 3}, -1) = T'(\mathbf{5}, -1)$

Try It Plot the image of △*RST* on the coordinate plane in Example 2 by translating it 2 units up. Label your point *R''* *S''* and *T''*.

d. What are the coordinates of *R''*? _____ Of *S''*? _____ Of *T''*? _____

Graphing Equations

You can use the coordinate plane to graph equations with two variables. A **T-table** can show various solutions to an equation.

Example

Graph the equation $y = x + 5$.

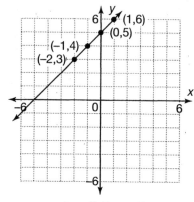

Step 1: Make a T-table for four values of x and y that will solve the equation.

x	y
-2	3
-1	4
0	5
1	6

Step 2: Plot the point for each pair of (x, y) values on the coordinate plane.

Step 3: Draw a line connecting the points. This line represents all the other values for x and the matching y values that make the equation true. This line is the graph of the equation $y = x + 5$.

Try It Graph the equation $y = 3x$.

a. Make a T-table for four values of x.

x	y
-1	
0	
1	
2	

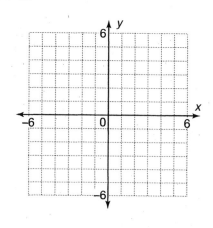

b. Plot the points on the coordinate plane.

c. Draw a line to connect the points.

Graph the equation $y = x - 5$.

x	y
0	
1	
3	
5	

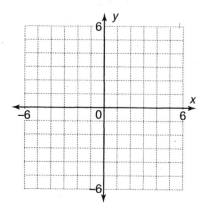

What is a Ratio?

A **ratio** is a comparison of two quantities. The ratio of Xs to Os in the box can be written as 4 to 3, 4:3, or $\frac{4}{3}$.

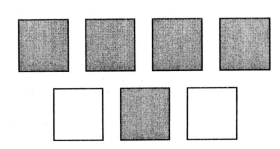

Like fractions, ratios can be rewritten in lowest terms.

══ Example 1 ══

Give a ratio comparing the number of shaded squares to white squares.

There are five shaded squares and two white squares.

The ratio of shaded squares to white squares can be written as 5 to 2, 5:2, or $\frac{5}{2}$.

Try It Use the letters in the box.

A	C	C	C	L	L	L	L	L
O	O	O	R	R	R	R	R	

a. How many letters in all? _____

b. How many letters are Rs? _____   **c.** How many letters are Os? _____

d. Give the ratio of Rs to Os. _____   **e.** Give the ratio of Os to all letters. _____

══ Example 2 ══

Give a ratio comparing the number of obtuse angles to acute angles. Write this ratio in lowest terms.

There are two obtuse angles and four acute angles.

Write the ratio. To rewrite in lowest terms, divide numerator and denominator by the same number.

Simplify.

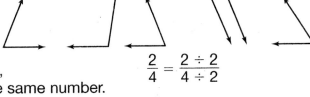

$$\frac{2}{4} = \frac{2 \div 2}{4 \div 2}$$

$$= \frac{1}{2}$$

In lowest terms, the ratio can be written as 1 to 2, 1:2, or $\frac{1}{2}$.

Try It Use the circles pictured. Write each ratio in lowest terms.

f. Give the ratio of dotted figures to striped figures. _____

g. Give the ratio of all figures to white figures. _____

h. Give the ratio of striped figures to all figures. _____

i. Give the ratio of striped figures to white figures. _____

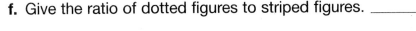

Name _____

Equal Ratios

You can find ratios that are equal to a known ratio by multiplying or
dividing both quantities of the ratio by the same amount.

━━ Example 1 ━━

Using multiplication, find four ratios equal to $\frac{1}{5}$.

Set up a table.

	×2	×3	×4	×5
1	2	3	4	5
5	10	15	20	25

Four ratios equal to 1:5 are 2:10, 3:15, 4:20, and 5:25. Other answers
are possible.

Try It   Find four ratios equal to each ratio by using multiplication to
complete the tables. Then write the ratios to the right of the table.

a.
3				
8				

_____

b.
1				
6				

_____

━━ Example 2 ━━

Using division, find four ratios equal to $\frac{48}{72}$.

Set up a table.

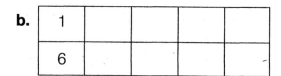

	÷2	÷3	÷4	÷6
48	24	16	12	8
72	36	24	18	12

Four ratios equal to 48:72 are 24:36, 16:24, 12:18, and 8:12. Other
answers are possible.

Try It   Find four ratios equal to each ratio by using division to complete
the tables. Then write the ratios to the right of the table.

a.
80				
100				

_____

b.
75				
150				

_____

What Is a Rate?

Some ratios are know as **rates.** A rate is a comparison of two quantities with different units of measure, such as $\frac{60\text{ mi}}{1\text{ hr}}$. If the comparison is to 1 unit, the rate is called a **unit rate.** Find equal rates by multiplying or dividing both quantities by the same number.

━ Example 1 ━

State if the ratio $\frac{3\text{ apples}}{\$5}$ is a rate.

The ratio is a rate because the measures are in different units.

Try It If the ratio is a rate, write *rate.* If it is not, write *ratio.*

a. 5 circles to 2 circles _____

b. 24 packages per carton _____

c. 5 dogs:8 cats _____

d. 3 teaspoons to 1 teaspoon _____

━ Example 2 ━

State if the rate 45 students in two classrooms is a unit rate.

The ratio is a *not* a unit rate because the comparison is to 2 classrooms. To be a unit rate the comparison must be to one unit.

Try It If the ratio is a unit rate, write *unit rate.* If it is not, write *rate.*

e. 36 inches to 3 feet _____

f. 20 quarters in $5 _____

g. 12 eggs in a dozen _____

h. 25 miles per gallon _____

━ Example 3 ━

Ingrid runs 15 miles every 7 days. Use a table to find three more rates describing this situation.

		×2	×3	×4
Miles Run	15	30	45	60
Days	7	14	21	28

Three rates are $\frac{30\text{ miles}}{14\text{ days}}$, $\frac{45\text{ miles}}{21\text{ days}}$, $\frac{60\text{ miles}}{28\text{ days}}$.

Try It Miguel has 90 minutes of softball practice every 3 days. Use a table to find three more rates describing this situation.

Minutes	90			
Days	3			

i. _____

What Is a Proportion?

For two ratios, a **cross product** is the result of multiplying the top value in one ratio by the bottom value in the other.

A **proportion** is a pair of equal ratios. Units of measurement must be the same across the top and bottom *or* down the left and right sides. In a proportion the cross products of the two ratios are equal.

━━ Example 1 ━━

Find the cross products for the ratios $\frac{3 \text{ ft}}{5 \text{ sec}}$ and $\frac{12 \text{ ft}}{20 \text{ sec}}$.

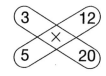

Multiply the top value of the first ratio and the bottom value of the second ratio.

$3 \times 20 = 60$

Multiply the bottom value of the first ratio and the top value of the second ratio.

$5 \times 12 = 60$

The cross products are 60 and 60.

Try It Find the cross products for each pair of ratios.

a. $\frac{3}{9}$ and $\frac{4}{12}$

$3 \times \underline{\hspace{1cm}} = \underline{\hspace{1cm}}$

$9 \times \underline{\hspace{1cm}} = \underline{\hspace{1cm}}$

b. $\frac{5}{8}$ and $\frac{3}{5}$

$\underline{\hspace{1cm}} \times \underline{\hspace{1cm}} = \underline{\hspace{1cm}}$

$8 \times \underline{\hspace{1cm}} = \underline{\hspace{1cm}}$

c. $\frac{4}{10}$ and $\frac{6}{15}$

$\underline{\hspace{1cm}} \times \underline{\hspace{1cm}} = \underline{\hspace{1cm}}$

$\underline{\hspace{1cm}} \times \underline{\hspace{1cm}} = \underline{\hspace{1cm}}$

━━ Example 2 ━━

State whether or not the ratios form a proportion.

Find the cross products for the ratios
$\frac{6 \text{ minutes}}{3 \text{ minutes}}$ and $\frac{12 \text{ feet}}{6 \text{ feet}}$.

The cross products are equal, so the ratios form a proportion.

Try It Find the cross products. Then state whether or not the ratios form a proportion. Write *yes* or *no*.

d. $\frac{4}{5} \overset{?}{=} \frac{2}{3}$

$4 \times \underline{\hspace{1cm}} = \underline{\hspace{1cm}}$

$5 \times \underline{\hspace{1cm}} = \underline{\hspace{1cm}}$

_____

e. $\frac{10}{50} \overset{?}{=} \frac{2}{10}$

$\underline{\hspace{1cm}} \times \underline{\hspace{1cm}} = \underline{\hspace{1cm}}$

$50 \times \underline{\hspace{1cm}} = \underline{\hspace{1cm}}$

_____

f. $\frac{9}{12} \overset{?}{=} \frac{6}{8}$

$\underline{\hspace{1cm}} \times \underline{\hspace{1cm}} = \underline{\hspace{1cm}}$

$\underline{\hspace{1cm}} \times \underline{\hspace{1cm}} = \underline{\hspace{1cm}}$

_____

Solving Proportions Using Cross Products

If you know one measurement and the ratio that the known and unknown measurement should have, you can write a proportion. Then you can use mental math or division to find the value of the unknown measure.

▬ Example 1 ▬

Use mental math to solve the proportion $\frac{4}{8} = \frac{3}{a}$.

Write the cross products as an equation.	$4a = 8 \times 3$
Multiply.	$4a = 24$
Think: What number times 4 equals 24?	$a = 6$

So, the proportion is $\frac{4}{8} = \frac{3}{6}$.

Try It   Write an equation for each proportion. Then use mental math to solve.

a. $\frac{1}{4} = \frac{b}{12}$

b. $\frac{5}{c} = \frac{35}{49}$

c. $\frac{d}{3} = \frac{18}{27}$

_____ = _____

_____ = _____

_____ = _____

$b =$ _____

$c =$ _____

$d =$ _____

▬ Example 2 ▬

Use division to solve the proportion $\frac{2}{6} = \frac{1.5}{e}$.

Write the cross products as an equation.	$2e = 6 \times 1.5$
Multiply.	$2e = 9$
Use division to undo the multiplication.	$e = 9 \div 2$
Simplify.	$e = 4.5$

So, the proportion is $\frac{2}{6} = \frac{1.5}{4.5}$.

Try It   Write an equation for each proportion. Then use division to solve.

d. $\frac{6}{10} = \frac{f}{12}$

e. $\frac{5}{g} = \frac{6}{36}$

f. $\frac{h}{9} = \frac{7}{12}$

_____ = _____

_____ = _____

_____ = _____

$f =$ _____

$g =$ _____

$h =$ _____

Solving Proportions Using Unit Rates

A unit rate is a ratio where one quantity is compared to exactly one unit of another quantity. You can use division to find the unit rate.

Unit rates can be used to solve proportions. Find the unit rate of the given proportion, and use multiplication to find the unknown value.

▬ Example 1 ▬

Find the unit rate of $\dfrac{\$24}{10 \text{ paintbrushes}}$.

Divide by the unit quantity.

$$\dfrac{\$24 \div 10}{10 \text{ paintbrushes} \div 10}$$

Simplify.

$$= \dfrac{\$2.40}{1 \text{ paintbrush}}$$

So, the unit rate is $2.40 for one paintbrush.

Try It Find the unit rate for each.

a. $\dfrac{\$45}{9 \text{ hours}} = \dfrac{45 \div \rule{1cm}{0.15mm}}{\div} = \rule{2cm}{0.15mm}$

b. $\dfrac{300 \text{ miles}}{15 \text{ gallons}}$ _____

c. $\dfrac{48 \text{ cars}}{4 \text{ trailers}}$ _____

▬ Example 2 ▬

Use unit rates to solve the proportion $\dfrac{\$60}{12 \text{ pounds}} = \dfrac{?}{15 \text{ pounds}}$.

Divide to find the unit rate.

$$\dfrac{\$60 \div 12}{12 \text{ pounds} \div 12} = \dfrac{\$5}{1 \text{ pound}}$$

Multiply the unit rate by the number of pounds. $5 per pound $\times$ 15 pounds = $75

So, it would cost $75 for 15 pounds.

Try It Use unit rates to solve each proportion.

d. $\dfrac{6\,c}{3 \text{ gal}} = \dfrac{?\,c}{25 \text{ gal}}$

$$\dfrac{c \div \rule{1cm}{0.15mm}}{\text{gal} \div \rule{1cm}{0.15mm}} = \dfrac{c}{1 \text{ gal}}$$

_____ c per gal $\times$ 25 = _____ gal

So, $\dfrac{6\,c}{3 \text{ gal}} = \dfrac{c}{25 \text{ gal}}$

e. $\dfrac{360 \text{ mi}}{12 \text{ wk}} = \dfrac{? \text{ mi}}{5 \text{ wk}}$

$$\dfrac{\text{mi} \div \rule{1cm}{0.15mm}}{\text{wk} \div \rule{1cm}{0.15mm}} = \dfrac{\text{mi}}{1 \text{ wk}}$$

_____ mi per wk $\times$ _____ wk = _____ mi

So, $\dfrac{360 \text{ mi}}{12 \text{ wk}} = \dfrac{\text{mi}}{5 \text{ wk}}$

Similar Figures

Figures with the same size and shape are *congruent*. The symbol ≅ means "is congruent to."

Figures that have the same shape but not necessarily the same size are **similar** figures. The symbol ~ means "is similar to."

If two figures are similar, their matching angles have the same measure and their matching sides are proportional.

━━ Example 1 ━━

State whether the polygons appear to be congruent, similar, or neither.

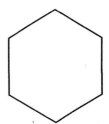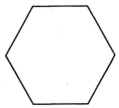

The figures are the same shape and size.

So, they are congruent.

Try It State whether the polygons appear to be congruent, similar, or neither.

a.

b.

_____   _____

━━ Example 2 ━━

△*ABC* ~ △*DEF.* Find the length of the side labeled *k.*

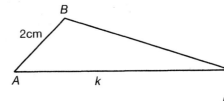

The triangles are similar, so the matching sides are proportional.

Write a proportion using the sides that match each other. $\dfrac{k}{3} = \dfrac{2}{1}$

Write the cross products. $k = 3 \times 2$

Multiply to solve for *k.* $k = 6$

So, the side labeled *k* measures 6 cm.

Try It △*GHI* ~ △*JKL.* Find the missing side lengths.

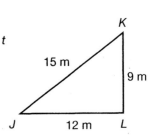

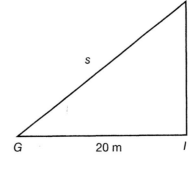

d. Write a proportion using sides that match. _____

e. Solve for *s.* _____

f. Solve for *t.* _____

Name _____

Alternative Lesson 10-8

What Is a Percent?

A **percent** is a ratio that compares a part to a whole using the number 100. The percent is the number of hundredths that the part is equal to.

━━ Example 1 ━━

Give the percent of the figure that is shaded.

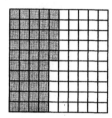

45 of the 100 squares are shaded. $\frac{45}{100} = 45\%$

So, 45% of the figure is shaded.

Try It Give the percent of each figure that is shaded.

a. 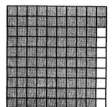 b. 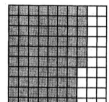 c. 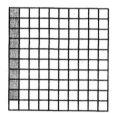 d.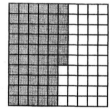

_____   _____   _____   _____

━━ Example 2 ━━

Give the percent of the figure that is shaded.

Each shaded section is $\frac{1}{4}$, or 25%, of the figure. Three sections are shaded, so the percent is 3 × 25%, or 75%.

So, 75% of the figure is shaded.

Try It Give the percent of the figure that is shaded.

e. What fraction describes each section? _____

f. What percent describes each section? _____

g. How many sections are shaded? _____

h. What percent is shaded? _____

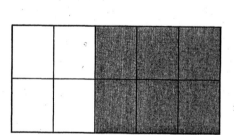

Give the percent of each figure that is shaded.

i.    j. 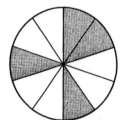   k.    l.

_____   _____   _____   _____

Estimating Percents

When estimating a percent, think of a fraction close to the given value
that uses halves, fourths, or tenths. These fractions can easily be
expressed as percents: $\frac{1}{2}$ is 50%, $\frac{1}{4}$ is 25%, and $\frac{1}{10}$ is 10%.

━━ Example 1 ━━

Estimate what percent of the grid is shaded.

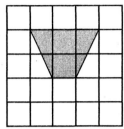

The trapezoid covers 2 squares completely.
It covers about $\frac{1}{2}$ of 4 more squares. Add to
estimate the total number of shaded squares.

$2 + \frac{1}{2} + \frac{1}{2} + \frac{1}{2} + \frac{1}{2}$, or 4 squares.

The total number of squares is 5×5, or 25.

The shaded part is about $\frac{4}{25}$, which is about $\frac{1}{5}$, or 20%.

About 20% of the figure is shaded.

Try It   Estimate what percent of each grid is shaded.

a.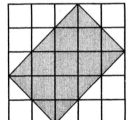

b.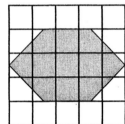

c.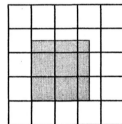

d.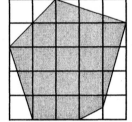

_____   _____   _____   _____

━━ Example 2 ━━

Estimate the percent: 32 out of 40.

32 is a little more than $\frac{3}{4}$ of 40.

So, 32 out of 40 is about 75%.

Try It   Estimate the percent.

e. 9 out of 91 is about what fraction? _____ What percent? _____

f. 140 out of 300 is about what fraction? _____ What percent? _____

g. 2 out of 206 is about what fraction? _____ What percent? _____

h. 15 out of 45 _____   **i.** 23 out of 98 _____   **j.** 83 out of 105 _____

k. 298 out of 500 _____   **l.** 71 out of 97 _____   **m.** 4 out of 422 _____

Connecting Percents to Fractions and Decimals

Fractions, percents, and decimals all describe parts of a whole.
To convert a percent into a fraction or decimal, rewrite the percent
as a fraction over 100.

You can use a proportion to convert
a fraction into a percent.

$$\frac{\text{part}}{\text{whole}} = \frac{\text{percent value}}{100}$$

Example 1

Convert 15% to a fraction in
lowest terms and to a decimal.   To convert to a fraction.   To convert to a decimal.

Write the percent as a fraction
with a denominator of 100. $15\% = \frac{15}{100}$ $15\% = \frac{15}{100}$

Then rewrite in requested form. $= \frac{15 \div 5}{100 \div 5} = \frac{3}{20}$ $= 0.15$

So, $15\% = \frac{3}{20} = 0.15$.

Try It Convert to a fraction in lowest terms and to a decimal.

a. $67\% = \frac{}{100} = $ _____ = _____   b. $48\% = $ _____ = _____ = _____

c. $82\% = \frac{}{100} = $ _____ = _____   d. $35\% = $ _____ = _____ = _____

Example 2

Convert $\frac{1}{3}$ to a percent.

Write a proportion using the fraction and 100. $\frac{\text{part}}{\text{whole}} \rightarrow \frac{1}{3} = \frac{x}{100} \leftarrow \frac{\text{percent value}}{100}$

Find the cross products. $100 = 3x$

Use division to undo multiplication. $100 \div 3 = x$

Divide. Solve for x. $33\frac{1}{3} = x$

So, $\frac{1}{3} = 33\frac{1}{3}\%$.

Try It Convert to a percent.

e. Write a proportion. $\frac{4}{5} = $ ——   f. Find the cross products. _____ = _____

g. Write $\frac{4}{5}$ as a percent. _____   h. $\frac{12}{100} = $ _____

i. $\frac{30}{50} = $ _____   j. $\frac{26}{40} = $ _____

Finding a Percent of a Number

You can use a proportion to find a percent of a whole number or you can convert the percent to a decimal and multiply.

$$\frac{\text{part}}{\text{whole}} = \frac{\text{percent value}}{100}$$

▬ Example 1 ▬

Simplify 22% of 83.

Write a proportion.

$$\frac{\text{part} \rightarrow}{\text{whole} \rightarrow} \frac{x}{83} = \frac{22}{100} \frac{\leftarrow \text{percent value}}{\leftarrow \quad 100}$$

Find the cross products. $\qquad 100x = 1826$

Use division to undo multiplication. $\qquad x = 1826 \div 100$

Divide. Solve for x. $\qquad x = 18.26$

So, 22% of 83 is 18.26.

Try It Simplify 70% of 35.

a. Write 70% as a decimal. _____

b. Multiply the decimal and 35. _____

Simplify.

c. 55% of 55 _____

d. 84% of 75 = _____

e. 18% of 9 _____

f. 26% of 45 _____

g. 63% of 150 = _____

h. 99% of 350 _____

▬ Example 2 ▬

Find the total amount. 25% of ☐ is 98.

Write a proportion using the fraction and 100.

$$\frac{\text{part} \rightarrow}{\text{whole} \rightarrow} \frac{98}{x} = \frac{25}{100} \frac{\leftarrow \text{percent value}}{\leftarrow \quad 100}$$

Find the cross products. $\qquad 9800 = 25x$

Use division to undo multiplication. $\qquad 9800 \div 25 = 25x \div 25$

Divide. Solve for x. $\qquad 392 = x$

So, 98 is 25% of 392.

Try It Find the total amount. 16% of ☐ is 12.

i. Write a proportion. $\frac{12}{x} = $ _____

j. Find cross products. _____ = _____

k. 46% of what number is 14? _____

l. 80% of ☐ is 8 _____

m. 65% of ☐ is 13 _____

n. 4% of ☐ is 18 _____

o. 24% of ☐ is 6 _____

p. 60% of ☐ is 54 _____

q. 12% of ☐ is 66 _____

Name _____

Classifying Solids

A **solid** is a three-dimensional figure or a figure that takes up space. The flat surfaces of a solid are called **faces**. The line where two faces come together is an **edge**. The point where several edges come together is a *vertex*.

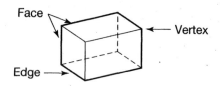

Face — Vertex
Edge

A solid whose faces are polygons is called a **polyhedron**. If two of the faces are parallel and congruent, the polyhedron is a **prism**. The parallel faces of a prism are the **bases**.

Base

Triangular Prism   Rectangular Prism   Pentagonal Prism

A **pyramid** is a solid with one base. All the other faces are triangles. Both prisms and pyramids can be named by the shapes of their bases.

Triangular Pyramid   Rectangular Pyramid   Pentagonal Pyramid

━━ Example ━━

Classify the solid. If it is a polyhedron, tell how many vertices, edges, and faces it has.

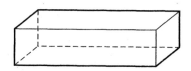

The solid is made up of flat surfaces, so it is a polyhedron.
It has two bases so it is a prism.
The bases are rectangles, so it is a rectangular prism.
There are 8 vertices, 12 edges, and 6 faces.
So, the figure is a rectangular prism with 8 vertices, 12 edges, and 6 faces.

━━ Try It ━━

Complete the table to classify each solid. If it is a polyhedron, tell how many vertices, edges, and faces it has.

Number of bases			
Shape of base			
Figure			
Vertices			
Edges			
Faces			

Name _____

Exploring Surface Area

The **surface area (SA)** of a polyhedron is the sum of the areas of all of its faces. To find the surface area of a polyhedron such as this rectangular prism, unfold it into a net of polygons and then add their areas.

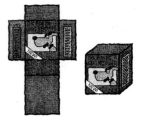

Like the area for a single polygon, surface area is measured in square units, such as cm^2.

▬ Example ▬

Find the surface area of the prism.

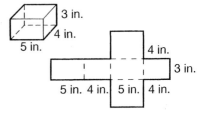

The net consists of 2 rectangles with lengths of 5 in. and widths of 4 in., two 4 in.-by-3 in. rectangles, and two 5 in.-by-3 in. rectangles.

SA = area of 2 rectangles + area of 2 rectangles + area of 2 rectangles

$$
\begin{aligned}
SA &= 2 \times (5 \times 4) &&+ 2 \times (4 \times 3) &&+ 2 \times (5 \times 3) \\
&= 2 \times (20) &&+ 2 \times (12) &&+ 2 \times (15) \\
&= 40 &&+ 24 &&+ 30 \\
&= 94 \text{ in}^2
\end{aligned}
$$

The surface area of the rectangular prism is 94 in^2.

▬ Try It ▬

Find the surface area of the pyramid.

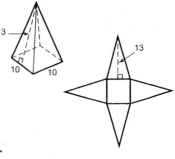

a. Which polygons make up the net? _____

b. Write an equation to find the area of the base.

_____

c. Write an equation to find the area of one triangular face.

_____

d. What is the area of four triangular faces? _____

e. Add to find the surface area. _____

Find the surface area of each solid.

f.

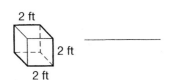
_____

g.

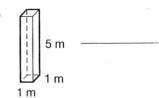
_____

Surface Area Formulas

When a polyhedron has congruent faces, you can use shortcuts
(formulas) to find the surface area.

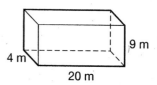
10 in.

5 in.

3 in.

━━ Example 1 ━━

Find the surface area of the prism.
l = 3 in., w = 5 in., h = 10 in.

Substitute the measures
into the formula (shortcut)
and solve.

$SA = (2 \times l \times w) + (2 \times l \times h) + (2 \times w \times h)$
$= (2 \times 3 \times 5) + (2 \times 3 \times 10) + (2 \times 5 \times 10)$
$= 30 + 60 + 100$
$= 190$

The surface area of the rectangular prism is 190 in^2.

Try It Find the surface area of the prism.
l = 20 m, w = 4 m, h = 9 m

a. Substitute the measures into the formula.

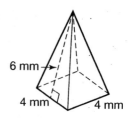
9 m

4 m

20 m

_____

b. Solve to find the surface area. _____

━━ Example 2 ━━

Find the surface area of the pyramid.

The base of the pyramid is a square measuring 4 mm
on a side. Each face is a triangle with a base of 4 mm
and a height of 6 mm.

6 mm

4 mm   4 mm

Substitute the measures into the formula (shortcut) and solve.

SA (pyramid) = area of base + [(number of triangular faces) $\times$ (area of each face)]
$= (4 \times 4) + [4 \times (4 \times 6 \div 2)]$
$= 16\ \ + [4 \times 12]$
$= 64$

The surface area of the pyramid is 64 mm^2.

Try It Find the surface area of the pyramid.

The base of the pyramid is a square measuring 10 m
on a side. Each face is a triangle with a base of 10 m
and a height of 15 m.

c. Substitute the measures into the shortcut.

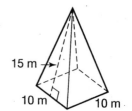
15 m

10 m   10 m

_____

d. Solve to find the surface area. _____

Surface Area of a Cylinder

A cylinder has two bases. Each base is a circle.
The side can be unrolled to form a rectangle.
The length of the rectangle equals the
circumference of the circle.

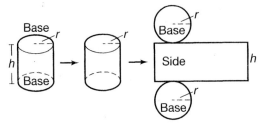

You can use these relationships to find the surface area of a cylinder
whose height is h and whose bases have a radius of r.

SA = (2 × area of base) + (area of rectangular side)
= (2 × area of base) + (height of side × length of side)
= (2 × area of base) + (height of cylinder × circumference of base)
= (2 × πr^2) + (h × 2πr)

━ Example ━

Find the surface area of the cylinder.
Use 3.14 for π. r = 4 m h = 8 m

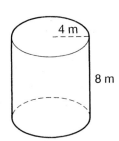

Substitute the measures SA = (2 × πr^2) + (h × 2πr)
into the formula   ≈ (2 × 3.14 × 4 × 4) + (8 × 2 × 3.14 × 4)
(shortcut) and solve.   ≈ 100.48 + 200.96
                            ≈ 301.44

The surface area of the rectangular prism is about 301.44 m².

Try It   Find the surface area of the cylinder.
Use 3.14 for π. r = 1 cm h = 4 cm

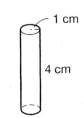

a. Substitute measures into the formula.

_____

b. Solve to find the surface area. _____

Find the surface area of the cylinder.
Use 3.14 for π. d = 6 in. h = 3 in.

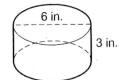

c. Divide the diameter by 2 to find the radius. _____

d. Substitute measures into the formula.

_____

e. Solve to find the surface area. _____

Name _____

Three-Dimensional Figures

Solids are often drawn in perspective to
show that they are three-dimensional.

Solids can also be drawn using a flat view.
Flat drawings show the solid from one view
only. In order to record what the solid looks
like, you usually need to show three views:
front, side, and top.

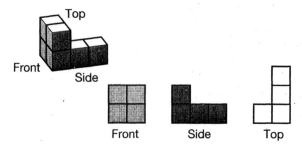

▬ Example ▬▬▬▬▬

Draw the front, side, and top views of the solid.
There are no hidden cubes.

Look at the position of the cubes that make up the
front view of the figure. There are two stacks of two
cubes each and one stack of one cube. Draw squares
to show each position.

Look at the position of the cubes that make up the side
view of the figure. There are three stacks of two cubes
each. Draw squares to show each position.

Look at the position of the cubes that make up the top
view of the figure. There are four stacks of two cubes
each and one stack of one cube. Draw squares to show
each position.

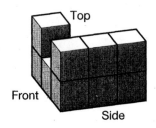

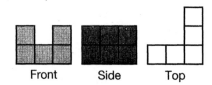

Try It Draw front, side, and top views of the solid.
There are no hidden cubes.

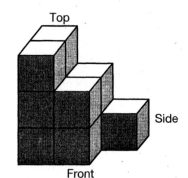

a. How many cubes make up the front view? _____

b. How many cubes make up the side view? _____

c. How many cubes make up the top view? _____

d. Draw the front view.   **e.** Draw the side view.   **f.** Draw the top view.

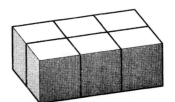

Exploring Volume

Three-dimensional objects can be measured by their volume. The **volume** of an object is the number of **cubic units** it contains. You can find the volume of a rectangular prism by counting cubes.

Volume = 6 cubic units

The exponent 3 means to use the base number as a factor 3 times.

5^3 (read "5 cubed") $= 5 \times 5 \times 5 = 125$

▬ **Example** ▬▬▬

Find the volume of the rectangular prism.

Each layer of the prism is 4 cubes by 5 cubes. This equals 4×5, or 20 cubes.

There are 3 layers in the prism. Multiply the number of layers by the number of cubes in each layer.

$3 \times 20 = 60$ cubes

The volume of the prism is 60 cubic units, or 60 units^3.

Try It Find the volume of the rectangular prism.

a. Write an equation to find the number of cubes in each layer.

b. How many layers are there? _____

c. Multiply to find the volume. _____

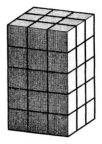

Find the volume of the rectangular prism.

d. Write an equation to find the number of cubes in each layer.

e. How many layers are there? _____

f. Multiply to find the volume. _____

Find the volume of each rectangular prism.

g.

h.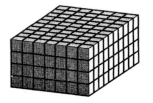

_____   _____

Name _____

Calculating Volume

You can use a formula to find the volume of a rectangular prism.
The volume is the product of the prism's length, width, and height.

Volume = length × width × height

━ Example ━

Find the volume of the rectangular prism.

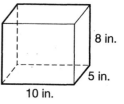

Find the measure of each dimension.
Length = 10 in. Width = 5 in. Height = 8 in.

Write the formula. $V = l \times w \times h$
Substitute the known values. $V = 10 \times 5 \times 8$
Multiply. $V = 400$

The volume of the prism is 400 cubic inches, or 400 in^3.

Try It Find the volume of the rectangular prism.

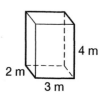

a. Write each measure.

Length _____ Width _____ Height _____

b. Substitute the values in the formula. $V =$

c. Find the volume. _____

Find the volume of the rectangular prism.

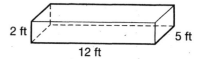

d. Write each measure.

Length _____ Width _____ Height _____

e. Substitute the values in the formula. $V =$

f. Find the volume. _____

Find the volume of each rectangular prism.

g.

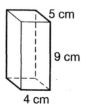

h.

i.

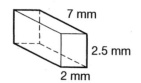

_____   _____   _____

Name _____

Probability

A probability **experiment** is a situation that can happen in more than one way. The **outcomes** of an experiment are the ways it can happen. For example, there are 2 outcomes–a head or a tail–if you toss one coin.

An **event** is the particular outcome that you're looking for. You can describe the **probability** that a particular event will happen by using a ratio.

$$P(event) = \frac{\text{number of ways the event can happen}}{\text{number of possible outcomes}}$$

It is sometimes helpful to express a probability as a decimal or percent.

━ Example ━

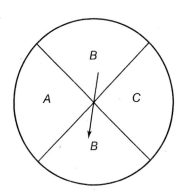

Write the probability of spinning A. Then express your answer as a decimal and a percent.

Each section on the spinner represents a different letter. All sections are the same size. Therefore, each outcome is equally likely to occur when you spin the spinner.

$P = \frac{1}{4}$ ← Number of ways the event can occur
        ← Possible outcomes: A, B, B, C

$\frac{1}{4} = 0.25$ or 25%

So, the probability of spinning A is $\frac{1}{4}$, 0.25, or 25%.

Try It   Suppose you toss a six-sided number cube. You want to roll an odd number.

a. How many equally likely outcomes are there? _____

b. How many ways can the event occur? _____

c. Write the probability of rolling an odd number as a fraction, a decimal, and a percent.

_____

Write each probability. Express each answer as a decimal and a percent.

d. What is the probability of spinning B
on the spinner in the example?   _____

e. A bag of buttons contains 4 red buttons,
4 blue buttons, 3 purple buttons, and
1 yellow button. What is the probability of
picking a purple button without looking?   _____

Making Predictions

Sometimes it is difficult to calculate the probability of an event because you don't know all the possible outcomes or you don't know how likely each outcome is. In these situations, you can sometimes collect data and predict the probability based on the data.

A **sample** is a set of data that can be used to predict how a particular situation might happen. You can use sample data to determine probability.

━━ Example ━━━━

The school cafeteria manager collected data to see what kind of snacks were chosen most often by the students. Based on this data, what is the probability that students will choose pretzels as a part of their lunch?

Type of snack	Number ordered
Potato	100
Corn	40
Tortilla	80
Cheese puffs	40
Barbecue	60
Pretzels	80

There were 400 bags of snacks chosen. Of the 400 bags, 80 bags were pretzels. So, the manager can expect $\frac{80}{400}$, or $\frac{1}{5}$, of the students to order pretzels.

Try It At Swann's Soda Shop, 7 students ordered vanilla shakes, 14 ordered chocolate shakes, and 9 ordered strawberry shakes.

 a. How many students ordered shakes? _____

 b. How many ordered vanilla shakes? _____

 c. What is the probability the next student will order a vanilla shake? _____

 d. What is the probability the next student will *not* order a vanilla shake? _____

Suppose you place cards showing the letters G A M E S into a sack.

 e. How many cards are there? _____

 f. How many cards show letters that are vowels? _____

 g. What is the probability that, without looking, a student will draw a card showing a vowel? _____

Geometric Models of Probability

Some events and outcomes are not always single items that can be counted. For situations such as carnival games and dart boards, the probability of an event happening depends upon the areas of portions of a figure. If you can determine each area within the figure, you can determine the probability of the situation.

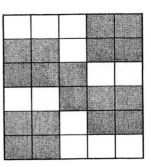

▬ Example ▬

A carnival game has a dart board with a pattern like the one at the right. What is the probability of hitting a shaded square?

There are 30 square units in the rectangle. 18 of them are shaded. The probability of hitting a shaded square is $\frac{18}{30}$ or $\frac{3}{5}$.

Try It Use the game board to find each probability.

a. What is the probability of a marker landing on the letter *W*? _____

b. What is the probability of a marker landing on the letter *O*? _____

c. What is the probability of a marker landing on the letter *R*? _____

d. What is the probability of a marker landing on the letter *D*? _____

R	W	O	D
D	O	W	O
D	R	R	W
W	R	D	R

Suppose you drop a token on each shape. Find the probability of the token landing on the shaded area.

e.
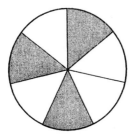
_____

f.
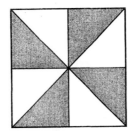
_____

g.
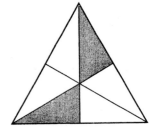
_____

A skydiver jumps out of a plane above an area represented by the map.

h. What is the probability the skydiver will land in water? _____

i. What is the probability the skydiver will land on land? _____

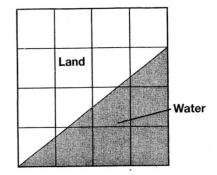

Tree Diagrams

It is often easy to list the outcomes for a single experiment. It can be more complicated to list the outcomes for a series of experiments. To list the outcomes for a series of experiments, you can use a **tree diagram.** A tree diagram shows one branch for each possible outcome.

▬ Example ▬▬▬

Janice has two skirts (one is red; the other is blue). She has three blouses (one is striped; one is plaid; one has polka dots). How many different outfits can she make?

List the choices for skirts.

List the choices for blouses.

List all possible choices.

Red
- Striped ——— Red skirt, striped blouse
- Plaid ——— Red skirt, plaid blouse
- Polka dot ——— Red skirt, polka dot blouse

Blue
- Striped ——— Blue skirt, striped blouse
- Plaid ——— Blue skirt, plaid blouse
- Polka dot ——— Blue skirt, polka dot blouse

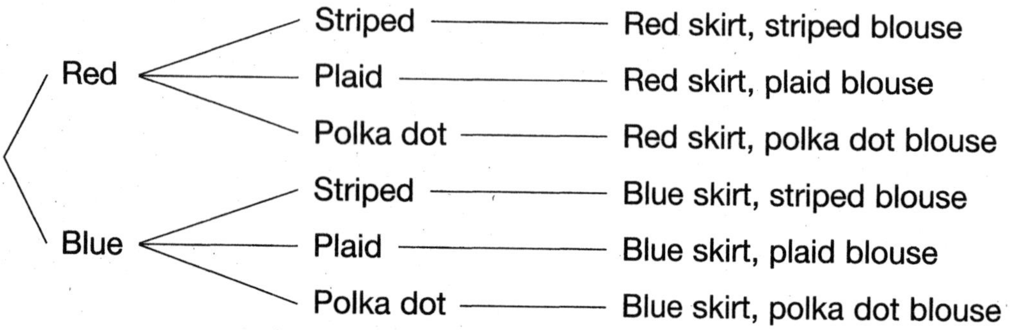

Janice can make 6 different outfits.

Try It At a card shop, Ernie has his choice of birthday balloons (confetti, flowers, or bears) and his choice of ribbon colors (purple and green). Draw a tree diagram to show all of the possible combinations of balloons and ribbons.

List the choices for balloons.

List the choices for ribbons.

List all possible choices.

Compound Events

A single event is the outcome of a single experiment, such as tossing a coin and getting heads. A **compound event** is a combination of two or more single events, such as tossing a coin and getting heads *and* then rolling a 6 on a number cube.

To find the probability for a compound event, first calculate the number of possible outcomes. Then calculate the number of ways the compound event can happen. The probability is the ratio of these values.

▬ Example ▬

What is the probability of spinning an even number on Spinner 1 and an odd number on Spinner 2?

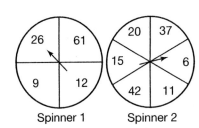
Spinner 1   Spinner 2

Find the number of possible outcomes for each spinner.

Spinner 1: 26, 61, 9, 12 → 4 outcomes
Spinner 2: 20, 37, 6, 11, 42, 15 → 6 outcomes

Multiply to find the total number of possible outcomes:
4 × 6, or 24 possible outcomes.

Determine the number of ways to get an even number for Spinner 1 and an odd number for Spinner 2.

Spinner 1, even number: 26, 12 → 2 ways
Spinner 2, odd number: 15, 37, 11 → 3 ways

Multiply to find the number of ways: 2 × 3 = 6.

So, the probability is $\frac{6}{24}$, or $\frac{1}{4}$.

Try It Find the probability of spinning a triangle on Spinner A and a pentagon on Spinner B.

a. How many possible outcomes are there?

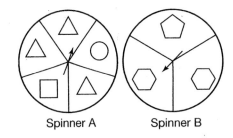
Spinner A   Spinner B

_____

b. How many ways can you spin a triangle on Spinner A? _____

c. How many ways can you spin a pentagon on Spinner B? _____

d. What is the probability of spinning a triangle and a pentagon? _____

Use Spinners A and B for the following exercises.

e. Find the probability of spinning a circle on A and a hexagon on B. _____

f. Find the probability of spinning a triangle on A and a hexagon on B. _____

g. Find the probability of spinning a square on A and a triangle on B. _____

Fairness and Unfairness

A game is **fair** if each player has the same probability of winning. The game is **unfair** if one player has a greater probability of winning. You can determine if a game is fair or unfair by comparing the probabilities for winning.

▬ Example ▬

In a game, 2 counters are tossed. One side of each counter is black and the other side is white. Player A wins if the colors are the same and Player B wins if the colors are different. Is the game fair?

There are 2 outcomes for each cube. Since there are two cubes, there are 2×2 or 4 possible outcomes.

Player A wins if both counters are black or if both are white. The probability of Player A winning is $\frac{2}{4}$, or $\frac{1}{2}$, or 50%, so the game is fair.

Try It There are 4 green buttons and 8 blue buttons in a bag. Player A wins if a green button is pulled out. Player B wins if a blue button is pulled out.

a. How many possible outcomes are there? _____

b. In how many ways can Player A win? _____

c. In how many ways can Player B win? _____

d. What is the probability of Player A winning? _____

e. What is the probability of Player B winning? _____

f. Is the game fair or unfair? Explain. _____

_____

Decide if each is a fair or unfair game. Explain.

g. A twelve-sided number cube is rolled. Player C wins if the number rolled is even. Player D wins is the number rolled is odd.

_____

h. Three coins are tossed. Player E wins if 1 head and 2 tails are tossed. Player F wins if 3 tails are tossed.

_____

_____